THE CELTIC CHURCH IN WALES

The Celtic Church in Wales

Siân Victory

LONDON
SPCK

First published 1977
SPCK
Holy Trinity Church
Marylebone Road
London NW1 4DU

Filmset in 'Monophoto' Ehrhardt 11 on 13 pt by
Richard Clay (The Chaucer Press), Ltd, Bungay, Suffolk
and printed in Great Britain by
Fletcher & Son Ltd, Norwich

ISBN 0 281 02945 8

For my parents

Contents

List of Illustrations   ix

Acknowledgements   xi

Notes on References   xii

1   Historical Background   1

2   The Christian Sites   22

3   Church Organization   45

4   The Church within Society   64

5   Church Economy   89

6   Cultural Achievements   100

Notes   130

Suggestions for Further Reading   139

Suggestions for Places to Visit   141

Index   143

List of Illustrations

COVER

THE CHURCH AT PARTRISHOW, BRECONSHIRE

This early medieval church is full of interest, for its rood-screen, wall-paintings and other treasures escaped desecration in Cromwellian times. But the site was in use well before the medieval period: an eleventh-century font is preserved in the church, and the holy well of St Issui, who allegedly founded the site in the early days of the Celtic Church, lies beside the little stream below the church. The ancient chapel adjoining the west end of the church may have been built on the site of its Celtic forerunner; in the fourteenth century this chapel, superseded in its turn by the present church, was converted into a hermitage. In the church-yard to the south of the church, commanding a superb view over the surrounding countryside, is a medieval preaching-cross at which Archbishop Baldwin is said to have preached the Third Crusade when he passed this way (accompanied by Giraldus Cambrensis) towards the end of the twelfth century. Stone seats built against the outside wall of the church face the cross, and open-air services are still occasionally held here, following the tradition of open-air worship that goes back to the earliest days of the Celtic Church, and ultimately beyond then into pagan times.

PLATE I: CHRISTIAN STONE MONUMENTS   *Facing p. 52*

(a) An early memorial stone: Maen Madoc, which stands in its original position beside the Roman road from the fort (Y Gaer) at Brecon to the coast near Neath. The stone bears a Latin inscription commemorating Dervacus, son of Justus. Detail reproduced by permission of the National Museum of Wales.

(b) A tenth- or eleventh-century stone in the church at Llanhamlach, Breconshire, bearing a symbolic representation of the Crucifixion.

PLATE II:

A SCULPTED CROSS FROM MARGAM, GLAMORGAN

Facing p. 53

This massive disk-headed cross is a characteristic product of the tenth-
to eleventh-century Glamorgan school of ecclesiastical stone sculpture.
The figures of St John and the Virgin flank the cross-shaft, and an
inscription records that Conbelin sponsored the monument. The cross is
now in the Margam Stones Museum. Reproduced by permission of the
National Museum of Wales.

PLATE III:

LATE EXAMPLES OF
CELTIC ECCLESIASTICAL STONE CARVING   *Facing p. 84*

(a) The font at Newborough, Anglesey.

(b) The monument at Llanfihangel-y-traethau, Merionethshire, commemorating the mother of the church's twelfth-century founder.

PLATE IV: HOLY WELLS   *Facing p. 85*

(a) The well at Partrishow, with niches for offerings.

(b) A corner of the well at Llangybi, Caerns., showing the surrounding
ledge to accommodate pilgrims, and the steps by which sufferers seeking
cure could enter the water.

Acknowledgements

I am deeply grateful to Dr Kathleen Hughes, of Newnham College, Cambridge, who made many helpful suggestions, saved me from a number of errors, and kindly allowed me to refer to as-yet-unpublished work. My cousin, Philip Wyn Davies, of the National Library of Wales, Aberystwyth, very kindly looked up some references for me. Above all I am indebted to my husband, Louis, without whose encouragement the book would never have been completed. He provided much useful criticism, and he also took the majority of the photographs.

Thanks are also due to the University of Wales Board of Celtic Studies (History and Law Section) for permission to quote from *Vitae Sanctorum Britanniae et Genealogiae*, by A. W. Wade-Evans.

Note on References

CHRISTIAN STONE MONUMENTS

References are made to the numbering in V. E. Nash-Williams's indispensable catalogue, *The Early Christian Stone Monuments of Wales*, Cardiff 1950 (abbreviated N-W).

SAINTS' LIVES

Unless otherwise stated, quotations are taken from the following editions:

James, J. W., *Rhigyfarch's Life of St David*. Cardiff 1967.

Wade-Evans, A. W., *Vitae Sanctorum Britanniae et Genealogiae*. Cardiff 1944.

NAMES OF COUNTIES

For greater precision, the old county names have been used throughout, except where the modern counties, approximating to the ancient kingdoms, are more appropriate.

1

Historical Background

Wales did not exist when our story begins. When the exciting Eastern cult of Christ first gained a foothold in Britain, mainland Britain was under Roman occupation. The country was a jigsaw of tribal divisions, with one major divide: that between the highland zone of the north and west, and the lowland zone of the south-east. The Romans ruled these areas by military and civil government respectively.

To the Romans, Britain was at the ends of the earth. The highland areas in particular were an unpopular posting with the soldiers whose task it was to subjugate the unruly British, and to keep the Scots[1] and Picts at bay. Although the familiar, orderly layout of camps and roads existed here, as throughout the Empire, and although there were bath-houses and even an occasional theatre, this could not compensate for the remoteness, the dreary climate, and the hostility of the occupied highlands. South-east Britain, with its prosperous towns and villas, was luxurious by comparison.

Few of the British tribesmen of the hills would ever have travelled beyond their tribal area: in their narrow world, warfare was an aristocratic pursuit, a skirmish between the war bands of rival princes, in which honour and courage and loyalty were of far more importance than the nominal cause of the fight. The ways of the invaders must have seemed incomprehensible. Like African tribesmen in recent times, the British found their values undermined by colonists who did not play by the same rules. No amount of courage could compensate for their lack of organization and strategy: it would have taken a strong and united army to have blocked the Roman conquest. Like many an annexed people before and since, the highland British made their resentment felt by sporadic uprisings and persistent guerrilla warfare.

1

The British of the lowlands settled down more easily under the Roman yoke. Here the tribes were more prosperous and politically advanced, and they proved able to turn the occupation to their advantage, once initial resistance had failed. As had happened across the Channel, local administration remained in the hands of the native tribes, whose organization was restructured along Roman lines, with Roman-style towns serving as tribal capitals. Centrally heated villas sprang up, where but a few years previously the owners' families had been content with humble timber farmsteads. Tribal leaders assumed the new dignity of Roman civil office. The *pax Romana* made progress possible in industry and commerce.

Highland Britain, including most of Wales, was less deeply affected by these developments. Only among the Silures, the powerful tribe whose territory lay in south-east Wales, did Romanization make comparable progress, with numerous villas established on the fertile coastal plain and a sizeable tribal capital developed at Venta Silurum (Caerwent). But this area, the westward slopes of the Severn basin, is really a westward extension of lowland Britain, with little in common with the rough, less fertile, sparsely populated hills to the west.

Significantly, it is in this atypical area that we first hear of Christians within the modern border of Wales. The details of how Christianity spread to Britain are unknown, but by the third century at least some converts had been made. This was a century of danger for Christians: the temporal danger that professors of a faith promising a life after death could afford to scorn. In Britain, reputed martyrdoms include that of Aaron and Julian—of whom nothing is known except their names[2]—at the Roman legionary fortress of Isca (Caerleon), not far from Caerwent.

In the fourth century, Roman persecution of Christians at last came to an end, following the conversion of the Roman Emperor Constantine—though there were occasional setbacks. Now the Church faced new difficulties. Suddenly, its ranks were swelled by myriad converts; the organizational problems were immense. Important councils were held to determine Church policy, and British bishops were among those summoned to attend some of these councils, at Arles in 314, at Rimini in 359. But how well

2

established was Christianity in Britain by this time? What sort of people were the British Christians whom the bishops represented? Documentary evidence does not enlighten us; and if we turn to archaeology for the answers, there too the evidence is disappointingly sparse. Apart from portable objects, which may well have been moved from their original location, material evidence for Christianity in Roman Britain is limited to the south and east, with a few outlying finds in the area of Hadrian's Wall.

Already we have encountered the problem which hampers us throughout our study of the Celtic Church in Wales: shortage of evidence. There is very little material evidence for early Christianity in Wales right up until Norman times, with the notable exception of the 400 or so Christian stone monuments of fifth- to twelfth-century date which still survive from the days of Celtic Christianity. This shortage needs to be seen in context: evidence for the other aspects of life in western Britain during this period is even scarcer. The use of perishable materials—such as timber for buildings and utensils, leather for harness and boats and bottles, plant-fibres for baskets and fishing-nets—is one reason for this. As for written sources relevant to Christianity, these do exist, but are limited in scope. From the sixth century we have Gildas's *De Excidio*, a spirited denunciation of the conduct of the British during and after the Roman withdrawal, which includes a strong attack on the clergy. The *Life of St Samson*, the only genuinely early *Life* of a Welsh saint, is thought to be basically early seventh century in date. A small amount of early Church legislation survives, and there are some eighth-century grants recorded in the *Book of Lichfield*, while other charters, thought to be based on earlier records, are incorporated in the twelfth-century *Book of Llandaff* (a propagandist compilation designed to authenticate the antiquity and orthodoxy of the recently founded see of Llandaff). Some information on Church affairs can be gleaned from various historical writings: the ninth-century *Historia Brittonum* attributed to Nennius, and the *Life* of the English King Alfred written by the Welshman, Asser. Annals survive from a chronicle that was kept at St David's from the eighth century on. At the very end of the life of the Celtic Church, as Norman influence was more and more making itself felt, there was a sudden burst of literary activity: the *Lives* of the Welsh saints, except that of Samson, date from this time (the late eleventh and twelfth centuries), as does the *Book of Llandaff.*

Since we have to judge past cultures by the arbitrary standard of what has by chance survived the vicissitudes of weather, time, and decay, and by what (in a literate society) has been thought by contemporaries worthy of record, we inevitably form a distorted image. It may be tempting to fill in the gaps in our knowledge of Celtic Christianity from what we know of the later Church: but the Church that came to form an integral part of Celtic society can have borne little resemblance in its spiritual or material life to the Church of today. A society's ability to grasp and form concepts is governed by its own particular experience of life, and pre-Norman society in Wales was undeniably remote from any way of life which we ourselves have encountered. The same God, the same Gospel underlie Christianity now as then—but one has only to turn to an ancient biblical commentary to realize how radically the interpretation of those constant factors at the core of the Christian religion has changed.[3]

Returning with this caution in mind to the story of early Christianity in Britain, it seems reasonable to accept the fact that British bishops were invited to attend the Church councils as sufficient indication that in fourth-century Britain Christianity enjoyed a wider vogue than the chance finds of Christian objects would suggest. Naturally, we should not imagine that the British were converted overnight. In the mountainous areas in which we are interested, where fashions, even with the mass communication systems of today, lag far behind those of south-east Britain, paganism must have lingered especially long.[4] Indeed, we have proof of the continued vitality of British paganism (often hybridized with imported Roman beliefs), even in the lowland zone. Of the remains of Romano-Celtic temples from late Roman times that have been excavated in Britain, those at Lydney in Gloucestershire (in the Severn basin, of which the land of the Silures was a part) are of special interest to us. Some temples are just tiny shrines, but at Lydney we find an elaborate complex of buildings built within the ramparts of a hill-fort as a centre for healing, a pagan Lourdes. References in inscriptions to the god

Nodens show that it was no imported, alien god that was invoked here—Nodens is the god who appears in Welsh legend as the hero Lludd Llaw Ereint, in Irish as Núada. The temple at Lydney was built long after toleration of Christianity was decreed, and after British bishops were summoned to the councils at Arles and Rimini. The earliest date for its foundation would be A.D. 364.

It may be that the anti-Christian reaction under the apostate Emperor Julian prompted the building of some of the late temples. But Lydney, at any rate, attests no flash-in-the-pan reaction: the establishment survived into the fifth century. By then a defensive wall had had to be built around it, to protect it from the barbarian raiders who were hammering with ever-increasing strength on the vulnerable British shores. This was not a new threat in the west: it was apparently in the third century that Irish settlers—despite the adjustment of Roman defences to resist them—invaded and settled in considerable numbers in the south-west and north-west extremities of what is now Wales (that is, Dyfed, where a family of Irish descent continued to rule until the tenth century, and the Lleyn peninsula). Before long, the whole of Britain lay under concerted siege: in A.D. 367 Picts, Saxons, and Irish together swooped down upon Roman Britain and devastated a large part of the province. A temporary recovery followed, with new measures taken for defence. A naval commandant who dedicated a mosaic floor at the temple at Lydney was quite possibly attached to a fleet set up to patrol the Bristol Channel, with its headquarters at a new fort constructed at Cardiff. Yet Britain was, after all, no more than a remote outpost to the Romans. As the weakening Empire suffered onslaught from all sides, troops were withdrawn from Britain to defend more important lands and, less constructively, to fight the battles of upstart emperors overseas, including the Briton Magnus Maximus. The days of direct rule from Rome were numbered. In A.D. 406 the barbarian hordes crossed the Rhine; in 410 the Goths sacked Rome. Soon afterwards the British were told to see to their own defence. They seem to have managed surprisingly well, despite the withdrawal of the Roman administrators and of so many troops. New British kingdoms—perhaps deliberately

5

created as buffer-zones—emerged on the frontiers of what had been Roman Britain; and somehow these kept the Picts and Scots at bay.

However, other enemies were eventually to prove invincible: the Scandinavian and Germanic invaders—the Angles, Saxons, and Jutes. At first, in late Roman times, these people had come as mercenaries to towns such as Caerwent, helping the inhabitants to ward off other foes. But as the Romans departed, so the Anglo-Saxons migrated to Britain in ever-growing numbers, until all the most desirable, fertile regions lay in their hands.

This was no instant conquest, like that of the Normans at Hastings six hundred years later; nor were the invaders sufficiently organized to overrun all the land previously ruled by Rome. In retrospect, the fact that a formidable kingdom, England, was to grow from the small, scattered early settlements of adventurers seems wholly unsurprising, even predestined. But only the most pessimistic of British contemporaries could have foreseen this. Though the British could not evict the invaders, they did manage to hinder and restrict their advance. The Anglo-Saxons did not conquer the area that is now Wales, and it was not until the eighth century that they had pushed far enough westwards for the boundary between them and the British to be settled at more or less the modern boundary between England and Wales.

When the Saxon advance was so gradual, it is unrealistic to imagine that the Romanized way of life to which many Britons had become accustomed was snuffed out immediately the Saxons arrived on the scene. Continuity is increasingly being stressed by scholars of the period: continuity in occupation of some of the Romano-British towns; in certain areas, continuity in civil government; continuity in Latin literacy and learning; continuity in the Christian faith.

Early Christian stone monuments and the testimony of a sixth-century British writer, Gildas, show that in western Britain Christianity was securely established by the late fifth to sixth century A.D. Some historians consider that this was one of the areas where the faith had lived on from Roman times; others credit Christian fugitives from the Saxon advance with spreading the faith to this remote and therefore perhaps still largely pagan region. Probably both continuity and refugees played some part; but other influences, too, were at work. Western Britain was no longer a cultural backwater. With the loss of south-eastern Britain to the barbarians, the focus of British culture had swung to the west, and the immediate post-Roman centuries were a time of active intercourse between the various Celtic peoples whose lands fronted on the Irish Sea.[5] Recently, finds of imported pottery have shown that the harbours of these lands were being visited by trading vessels from Gaul, and even from the Eastern Mediterranean. Thus, the western British were in direct contact with the very area where Christianity had been born. Some of the imported pottery is tableware stamped with Christian symbols; there are also storage-jars which probably served as containers for imports of oil and wine. Apparently the native princes had acquired a taste for Roman luxuries—but probably too some of the imports were intended not for the princes' tables but for use in the Christian sacraments.

The imported pottery is not the only sign that the British aristocracy (even in the highlands, where Romanization had been slight) were hankering after the superior culture they had been privileged to glimpse. In western Britain, power had returned to the native rulers in their hilltop strongholds; but at the same time we find, on fifth- to sixth-century memorial stones in Gwynedd, proud reference to Roman titles: a *medicus* (doctor) at Llangian, 'a citizen of Gwynedd and cousin of . . . [a] magistrate' at Penmachno.[6] Presumably these titles—like those of barons and dukes today—retained little of their original function: it was their status that counted.

One of our very few contemporary written sources for this period is an invective by a British scholar, Gildas, against the conduct of his fellow-countrymen.[7] Gildas's denunciation of several western British princes confirms the view that they had taken to Roman ways only on the most superficial level. Far from conforming to Roman standards of discipline, they are tyrants, he asserts, arrogant and perpetually indulging in squabbles, unable to put up a unified resistance to their common enemy, the Saxons. Gildas's viewpoint is heavily pro-Roman; before we echo his criticisms, we should remember that it was precisely the qualities he decries, the untamed vigour and aggressiveness of the princes, that enabled them to hold their own against the Saxon advance. The centuries of imposed Roman rule had left them as disunited as ever, but had not sapped their energy.

Thus, while the Saxon invasions were slowly swallowing up what remained of Romano-British culture in the south and east, western Britain was enjoying a cultural resurgence in which emulation of Roman ways, however superficial, was very much the fashion. Christianity was one of the borrowings. Like the Roman titles and pottery and wines, it was being imported into a world very different from that in which it had originated. Some adaptation to the different social and cultural surroundings was essential.[8]

The Roman Church belonged to an urban world; its organization echoed that of the efficient, centralized civil administration. At first the British Church, at least in the south-east, seems to have differed little from the Church on the Continent. In Constantius' *Life* of the Gaulish Bishop Germanus, written c.A.D. 480, we are told of two visits by Germanus to Britain (in A.D. 429 and 435) to crush an outbreak of Pelagian heresy:[9] he was met by native rhetoricians, splendidly dressed, and able to engage him in skilled debate. Here were affluent and accomplished clerics of the type found throughout the Church of the Western Empire, the ecclesiastical equivalents of the state dignitaries of the Roman provinces. As yet, it seems, the Saxon encroachment on the British lands had barely troubled them: they still had leisure for the niceties of theological argument. Somewhat later, Gildas's writings give much the same picture. He berates the British clergy for their worldliness and corruption; wrapped up in their own importance, they give too little attention to the souls of their flocks. The clergy were a social élite.

While Roman-style church organization may have been at home in the more Romanized lowlands of Britain, it could not be fitted without adjustment into the far less sophisticated society of the highlands. In western Britain there was no centralized administration upon which the Church could graft itself—only a multitude of minor chiefs and princes, with very limited power over the scattered population of peasants and pastoralists. But there was a new movement within the Church, which was far better suited to these conditions, and took its place alongside the Roman-derived hierarchy of clergy: monasticism.

Monasticism had developed in the Eastern Mediterranean lands in reaction to the very worldliness that Gildas deplored. Idealists such as St Anthony and St Jerome had fled to the desert to escape persecution and to pursue a religious life in solitude; and from these roots organized monasticism had grown. As independent, self-sufficient communities the early monasteries were ideally suited to survive in the unstable conditions following the disintegration of the Roman Empire—much more so than the urban-based hierarchy of priests and bishops.

In his attack on the clergy, Gildas makes exception of a very few truly holy men; and it is commonly held that he is referring to monks. As we have seen, western Britain was in direct trading contact with the Eastern Mediterranean and with Gaul—the lands where monasticism had been born and nurtured. Maybe monasticism was introduced into Britain by evangelists travelling to the British coast aboard the trading vessels—itinerant Christians sailing from port to port in the tradition of the Apostle Paul. Or maybe the new ideas were more casually spread. Some adventurous Britons must have put to sea with the departing ships, often to return at a later date filled with enthusiasm for what they had seen and heard abroad.[10] The receptivity of the British Church to developments overseas is seen from the use in many fifth- to sixth-century commemorative inscriptions of forms of wording currently fashionable in Gaul. Monasticism was able to take root in Britain at an early date.

However, Britain's contacts with the rest of the Christian world were at best sporadic. The barbarian influx into Gaul as well as into south-east Britain hampered Britain's connections with the continental Church. Overland communications were hazardous; ships were at risk from pirates; and though ships from North Africa and Gaul did sail to British ports, we should not suppose that their arrival was anything other than a rare event, to be spoken of with great excitement for many a year.

Contact was easiest with the other Celtic lands. It was in the late sixth century that the final wave of British emigrants is thought to have crossed to Brittany, from the south-west peninsula of Britain. There must have been a great deal of to-ing and fro-ing between the homeland and the new settlements, by priests and monks as well as by their lay kinsmen. Many of the distinguished Christians who became celebrated as saints in western Britain (in modern Wales and Cornwall) were also known in Brittany. Since Brittany is on the fringes of Gaul, some of the Gallic influence that affected the British Church may have arrived via Brittany.

Links with Ireland were equally close, but rather different in character. The Irish had their own speech and their own traditions; they had escaped the Roman occupation that had coloured the British outlook on life. For centuries they had been unwelcome intruders in Britain. Later traditions credited a North British prince, Cunedda, and his sons with expelling the Irish from much of what is now Wales; but Irish names in Welsh genealogies and the Irish inscriptions in Ogam on some of the early Christian monuments attest their continued presence, especially in Dyfed and the Brecon area, and their participation in the recently established British Church. British missionaries—most famous, St Patrick—played a part in the conversion of Ireland in the fourth to fifth centuries, and from then on the British and the Irish Churches kept in close touch. The Irish ecclesiastical vocabulary was built up by borrowings from British as well as continental Latin, while some specialized Irish terms later passed back to Britain, such as *secndab* (from Latin *secundus abbas*), used by the Irish for a deputy abbot destined to inherit the abbacy, borrowed as *segynnab* in Welsh. But the two Churches retained their individuality. By the sixth century, the Irish Church was restricting the activities of British clerics in Ireland;[11] and in Wales dedications to Irish saints are rare.[12]

The British Church was fortunate. Elsewhere in the former provinces of the Roman Empire the Church was all too often crumbling, like the society and economy that supported it. But the British Church was able to grow from strength to strength. Despite pressure from the Saxon invasions, this was not a time of universal destruction and despair in Britain. As Gildas tells us, the worst of reverses were soon forgotten; between bouts of localized warfare came long periods of peace, leaving the British princes free to pursue their own squabbles.

However, the comparative isolation of the British Church was to breed ill-feeling when, at the very end of the sixth century, missionaries from Rome arrived in Kent to fulfil Pope Gregory's dream of converting the Anglo-Saxons. Pope Gregory had been careful to give Augustine, the leader of the mission, no authority over the bishops he would meet *en route* in Gaul; but the British bishops were to Gregory an unknown—and therefore unrespected—quantity. They were commended to Augustine's care, 'so that the ignorant may be taught, the weak strengthened by persuasion, the perverse corrected by authority'.[13] Little wonder, then, that the missionaries' attempt to enlist the help of the British bishops and monks proved abortive, with the British (according to the English historian, Bede) baulking at Augustine's lack of humility.

Doubtless other factors contributed to the failure to co-operate. To the missionaries, accustomed to Roman standards of culture, and with their sympathies already soured by Britain's dreary climate and unfamiliar food, the British bishops—however splendid they thought themselves—can hardly have appeared other than outlandish. In turn, the British had every reason to be suspicious of a delegation which not only asked their help in converting their bitterest enemies, but ordered them to abandon ancient and respected customs of their church. For although the British had often eagerly copied whatever continental fashions had come to their notice, they had been out of touch with, or had chosen to ignore, some recent developments in the practice of the continental Church. Most controversial was to prove their failure to conform to the now widely accepted Roman method of calculating the date of Easter; but they were also adhering to outdated customs in other matters, including the form of the tonsure and the rite of baptism. Now Augustine was declaring that in following these time-honoured usages the British Christians were not simply old-fashioned, but were in error.

St Augustine's reaction to the breakdown of negotiations with the British Church was uncompromising: if the British would not accept peace from their brethren, he prophesied, they would have war from their enemies. Of course, such warfare had been in progress intermittently for the past two hundred years. The British would have found it hard to accept as brethren the barbarians who had relentlessly destroyed whatever of Christian culture they had encountered in their advance. Organized mission-work was still a novel idea: where one's enemies were concerned, it was a great advantage for them to be pagan. Then one could fight with the dedication of a holy war, and solace oneself in defeat with the smug knowledge of being a chosen people. Canons attributed to an early British church synod, the Synod of the Grove of Victory, impose relatively light penances for most offences; three years, for instance, for killing in anger. In sharp contrast, a Briton who serves as guide to the enemy is to do penance for thirteen years—but only if 'there does not ensue a slaughter of Christian folk and the shedding of blood and lamentable captivity'. Should these dire consequences follow, the culprit is to spend the rest of his life in penance.

The political gap between British and Anglo-Saxons was as yet far too wide for religion to bridge.[14] After the conversion of the Anglo-Saxons, the old conflict of pagan versus Christian became the equally bitter conflict of orthodox versus heretical—with both sides convinced that the orthodoxy was theirs. In the eighth century, an English scholar, Aldhelm, writing to King Geraint of Dumnonia (Devon and Cornwall) to urge him to bring his church to conform to Roman usage, complained that the British priests would not pray or eat with the English clergy, and that 'they throw out the food left over from our meals to dogs . . . and to foul pigs; they give orders that the dishes and bowls which we have used must be scraped and scoured with sand or with cinders before they are fit to be placed upon their tables.' The Saxons for their part refused to accept the ordination given by the British clergy as valid, and even Bede, a man of unusual integrity, was prepared to condone the massacre at Chester in the early seventh century by the pagan Northumbrians of some 1,200 unarmed British monks and priests, who had come to the scene of battle to pray for a British victory. To Bede, the slaughter was a just fulfilment of St Augustine's prophecy.

This story pinpoints the problem: how could the British and the Anglo-Saxon churches co-operate, when with every new skirmish they would be called upon—as were the monks at Chester—to pray for the success of their own people? But however inevitable, the resultant isolation of the British Church was to prove unfortunate. The converted Anglo-Saxons eagerly made use of their new contact with the rest of the Christian world—with Gaul, with Italy, with Byzantium. Greedily, the new Church drew upon all the cultural inspiration it could find: manuscripts and artwork, vestments and paintings, styles of building, the technique of glassmaking, and singing in the Roman manner were all imported into the Anglo-Saxon kingdoms. Stimulated by these, and by the art and scholarship introduced by Irish missionaries, the Anglo-Saxons swiftly evolved a distinguished Christian culture of their own. Once again, the focus of cultural activity in Britain had swung to the east. The British Church was in general cut off from these developments, except insofar as they filtered through to her by way of Ireland.

The Anglo-Saxon kingdoms were steadily growing from strength to strength. Their gains were consolidated; boundaries settled; any as yet unclaimed pockets of land swallowed up. It was in the later seventh century that the Mercians—originally a small group of settlers in the Trent valley—extended their territory until they occupied so broad a tract of land that the British were hemmed into what is now Wales.

Previously the British had had more to fear from the ambitious Northumbrian rulers—so much so that, in the mid-seventh century, King Cadwallon of Gwynedd had pooled his resources with those of the Mercian king, Penda, to defeat and slay the Northumbrian king, Edwin. Yet in doing so, Cadwallon, a Christian king, had allied himself with a pagan, Penda, to defeat Edwin, a Christian convert. Political expediency had triumphed over religious scruples—and of course the breach between the British and the Anglo-Saxon Churches helped make such expediency acceptable.

In A.D. 678 the Mercians finally put paid to Northumbrian expansion southwards by defeating the great Northumbrian king Ecgfrith at the Battle of the Trent. But British joy must have been short-lived, for it was then that the Mercians, relieved of danger from their Germanic neighbours, were for the first time free to concentrate their aggression on the British. There is no detailed record of the struggles that followed; but scattered dykes and ditches blocking routes into the Welsh mountains show how the Mercian pioneers who pushed forward into British territory were having to barricade their settlements against marauders from the hills. By the end of the eighth century, some sort of equilibrium had been reached. To mark the boundary hammered out between the two peoples, King Offa of Mercia had a grandiose earthwork constructed, the Dyke that now bears his name.[15] Determined by topographical as much as by political factors, the boundary has remained little changed down to the present day.

Interestingly, the alignment of Offa's Dyke is in places unfavourable to the Mercian interest; and the small earlier earthworks show that at times the Mercians had penetrated well beyond this boundary. It seems that the Dyke was a negotiated frontier. Peace, however uneasy, was surely in force when the Dyke was being built: even given the most favourable circumstances, the planning and construction of this 149-mile-long barrier was an amazing feat.

At last we can begin legitimately to talk of Wales, at least in a territorial sense. In other senses she was still not a discrete entity. Politically, her people remained local in outlook—loyal to their local rulers, not to any centralized power. Culturally, Wales shared in a wider British culture, reaching from Strathclyde in the north to what is now Cornwall in the south, and even further afield to Brittany. The Anglo-Saxons' westward advance had by now cut off the land-routes between the surviving British peoples, but contact by sea continued. Much of what we now consider as part of the Welsh heritage—much surviving legend and literature—in fact originated among the Northern British, the occupants of what is now southern Scotland. While the other North British kingdoms were one by one swallowed up by Northumbria, Strathclyde distinguished itself by holding on to its freedom, despite a ring of hostile neighbours—Northumbrians, Scots, and Picts. It is an accident of history that Wales today preserves more of its Celtic identity than its once vigorous northern cousin.

In A.D. 768 the Church in Wales finally conformed to the Roman method for calculating the date of Easter. Bishop Elfoddw of Gwynedd is credited with effecting the change; but he could have accomplished nothing had not the time been ripe. By now, the political boundary between the British and the Anglo-Saxons was relatively stable—this was the time of the construction of Offa's Dyke. The Church shared in the new security. It may seem paradoxical that, despite evidence for continued border warfare from the ninth century onwards, the ninth and especially the tenth centuries were a time of growing receptivity in Wales to foreign influences. The paradox disappears when one remembers that it is by opposition to outsiders that a people bolster their sense of identity; and the more confident they are of that identity, the more they can afford to accept change.

British scholars now took a new interest in their past and, unearthing what they could of old traditions, recorded them in written form. The native literature had been oral, preserved in the memories of the exhaustively trained story-tellers and bards. Now advantage was taken of church-introduced literacy to record some at least of the verses and prose in the Old Welsh language, much of it gleaned from North Britain. But ecclesiastics still enjoyed a virtual monopoly over the ability to read and write, and most of their writings continued to be in the Church's official language, Latin. In Gwynedd, the antiquarian Nennius was at work, uncritically collecting snippets of information about the British past. The ancestry of the more prominent Welsh princes was celebrated in elaborate written genealogies, and annalistic records were kept of notable events. It seems that the Church was now using its literacy for the entertainment of the aristocracy as well as for the edification of the clergy; for the glorification of the princes, as well as of God.

In the ninth century, King Rhodri of Gwynedd opened up new possibilities for British politics, by uniting almost the whole of Wales under his rule. The revival of old British traditions worked to his advantage, by presenting him as heir to the ancient glories of his line. It was the age-old function of the Celtic bard to uphold his patron's prestige by eloquent praise; now church scholars were fulfilling much the same role.[16] The dynasty of

Powys had already grasped the possibilities: capitalizing on the popularity in their kingdom of the cult of St Germanus,[17] they had fostered the story that it was through Germanus's intervention that they had acquired the throne. One doubts whether many churchmen would now have shared Gildas's view that the praise of princes was execrable, and the praises of God alone should be heard.

A new and terrible enemy was now harrying the Welsh coast: the Vikings. Persistent raiders of the wealthy churches, they were destroyers as well as plunderers: what they could not carry away with them they burnt. Yet it is an ill wind . . . King Rhodri was helped in his efforts to bring all the Welsh principalities under his rule by the people's need for a strong protector against the Vikings; and it could well be that the loss and destruction of many ancient possessions, including perhaps old records and books, helped stimulate the revival of interest in the past ages from which these now-vanishing treasures had been inherited.

Not just Wales, but the whole of the British Isles (and indeed much of western Europe) was under threat from the Norse and Danish adventurers. Hungry for food, for wealth, for the thrills of bloodshed, they swooped down on the coast in their swift ships, sailed up into the creeks and harbours, and seized produce and livestock and precious metals and women, and young, healthy people whom they could sell as slaves. Contemporaries recognized in their coming a judgement of God.

Rhodri's victories against the Vikings, like those of his Anglo-Saxon contemporary, King Alfred, contributed greatly to his renown. But whereas Alfred's successes paved the way for the creation of a united kingdom of England, Rhodri's efforts at unification came to nothing after his death. His inheritance, in the usual Welsh fashion, was divided between his sons. His widespread rule had been a personal triumph, not a political breakthrough. But he had unsettled the political structure; after his death no one quite knew where they stood, and his sons squabbled among themselves, and squabbled with other princes or claimants, till all Wales seethed with strife.

Now that both Welsh and Anglo-Saxons shared a common enemy, they could afford a new sympathy with each other. The

Welsh princes were quick to exploit the new friendliness, enlisting Anglo-Saxon help not only in campaigns against the Vikings but in their own internal rivalries. The Welsh annals allow us to glimpse the restless violence: in 894, for instance, Anaraut, Prince of Gwynedd, took English forces with him to ravage Ceredigion and Ystrad Tywi. The Welsh scholar, Asser, visited King Alfred to enlist his help against King Hemeid of Dyfed, who had expelled Bishop Nobis and his companions—including Asser—from St David's. Alfred eagerly recruited Asser to help him in his plan to restore learning in the wake of the Viking devastation; and Asser's colleagues agreed to his spending half each year at Alfred's court, because they saw the advantage of having Alfred as an ally.

So far, there was no question of the Welsh acknowledging any subordination to the Anglo-Saxons. After all, the Saxons had been all but engulfed by the Danes. But Alfred led them to recovery; and unlike those of Rhodri, Alfred's achievements were consolidated and built upon. Asser wrote a *Life of Alfred* which, even allowing for exaggeration, shows Alfred to have been a man of rare resourcefulness.[18] From co-operating with equals, the Welsh were all too soon to find themselves paying homage to superiors.

A Welsh poem, 'Armes Prydein',[19] shows that some at least of the Welsh soon came to recognize the danger. It foretells the day when the Welsh, Picts, Cornish, and British of Strathclyde will unite with the Danes based at Dublin to defeat the Saxons. At the battle of Brunanburh in 937 a coalition of the Scots, the men of Strathclyde, and the Dublin Danes did fight the Saxons—but lost. Quite possibly the poem was composed to rally support for this campaign. If so, it was unsuccessful, for many Welshmen preferred to keep the Saxons' friendship. One far-sighted Welshman, in particular, turned the growing English power to his own advantage. This was Hywel Dda. Hywel (who ruled from 918 to 952) succeeded in making himself king of all Wales, except the extreme south-east. He had a precedent to follow in his efforts at unification, other than Rhodri's transitory achievements; for under Alfred's successors a united Kingdom of England had been forged. Hywel was content to pay allegiance to Edward the

Elder, and later to Athelstan, kings of the new England, while at the same time he imitated the increased authority of the English kingship in his own kingdom. Not only did he aim to rule the whole of Wales, but he is credited also with ordering the codification of the Welsh Laws; and he issued coins bearing his name. By submitting to English power, he safeguarded his position. This left him free to nourish his kingdom's growth towards a more centralized and institutionalized society.

Hywel's vision was his alone. After his death Wales had no single heir, and yet again the political structure disintegrated, and the land was plagued by dissension and petty rivalries. A still more vigorous onslaught by the Vikings increased the chaos. Norsemen from the bases they had established in Ireland and the Isle of Man repeatedly ravaged the vulnerable coastline of Wales, especially the north-west and the south, which had in earlier centuries borne the brunt of the Irish raids and settlements. The Church remained a prime target: the same foundations would be raided time and time again. St David's is known to have been sacked four times just in the few years between A.D. 982 and 989. Not all the Viking raiders returned home. At first they settled in coastal camps which could serve as bases for future raids; later, they settled down permanently on the coast that appealed so strongly to these wanderers from the fjords. Their memory lives on in the Scandinavian names of many of the Welsh headlands and islands: Skokholm, Bardsey, Priestholm, Caldey, and the rest. The Vikings were not simply destroyers: raiding gave way to peaceful trade, and a few aspects of Celtic culture—stonecarving and metalwork in particular—benefited from the injection of new life from the alien Viking culture. But initially the Vikings did effect some measure of destruction; and they also disrupted Welsh society, both by fostering an atmosphere of insecurity (the approach of Saxon or British enemies, marching overland, could usually be detected in advance; but who knew when the Viking boats would drive in from the sea?), and by taking sides in local rivalries. For although the need for concerted opposition to the Vikings might strengthen the hand of those working towards Welsh unity, on the other side of the scales the Vikings could, and did, exploit the quarrels between the Welsh princes, ensuring

18

that the anarchy from which they benefited would persist.

Amazingly, the Church not only survived the long-lived and punishing onslaught of the Vikings, but, despite the loss of many resources—including men—maintained a reasonably high cultural standard. In the eleventh century, the work of the family of Bishop Sulien of St David's was outstanding. One son, Rhigyfarch, produced a polished Latin *Life of St David*; another, Ieuan, wrote and illuminated manuscripts. In the early twelfth century a spate of Latin *Lives* of the Welsh saints poured forth. But these owed something to yet another new arrival on the Welsh scene, the Normans.

Not long after the Battle of Hastings, the Norman conquerors of England turned their attention to their unruly western neighbour. Land- and power-hungry Norman lords—the Montgomeries and the de Braose family among them—carved out domains for themselves in Welsh territory, throwing up castles wherever they went to consolidate their hold. At first, the Welsh princes treated the Normans like their earlier enemies, as capable of manipulation to suit their own ends. In south-west Wales, Rhys ap Tewdwr paid homage to William the Conqueror to safeguard his challenged possession of the throne. But the Normans were a more formidable threat than the Welsh at first suspected: they were a devastatingly efficient war-machine, expert strategists, like the Romans before them—endowed with the very qualities that the disunited, impetuous Welsh lacked. After Rhys's death in 1093 the Normans surged into Wales, each lord working on his own behalf, but with equal skill at applying the techniques of conquest. Now at last the Welsh awoke to the danger, and revolts followed throughout Wales. But though the princes of the mountainous north and west regained their freedom, the Normans clung on to their conquests in the south and east. Already by the early twelfth century the Welsh were hemmed in by a hostile crescent of Marcher lordships, stretching southwards along the border from Chester, then sweeping west across the south Wales coastal plain to Pembroke. The north and west of Wales was like a stag at bay.

Within the March, Welsh life in the mountains and moorland continued little changed. It was the desirable lowland that the

Normans appropriated: this was parcelled out among the vassals of the great Marcher lords. Church lands were not immune. The Normans, whose violent lives left them much in need of divine favour, sought to buy it by generously endowing respected Norman abbeys. Breaking up the religious communities or *clasau* which they found at many of the Welsh churches, they handed over the endowments of these churches to abbeys in Normandy or England: St Peter's of Gloucester, for instance, was favoured with many endowments in Glamorgan.

Like recent imperialists in Africa and the East, the Normans had a ready excuse for their high-handed actions. The Welsh Church, they claimed, was debased and corrupt. Doubtless in many respects these criticisms were just. Although the breach with the Roman Church over the date of Easter had been healed, the Celtic churches had retained their own customs in many respects.[20] Judged by the strict discipline of the reformed Roman Church, some of their practices were lax indeed; and their lack of a centralized organization left room for considerable variation in standards. In contemporary Scotland and Ireland the same need for reform was recognized.

The Normans secured control over the Welsh Church through its administrative heads, the bishops. By the mid-twelfth century, all four bishops in Wales—those of Bangor, St Asaph, St David's, and Llandaff—had professed obedience to the Archbishop of Canterbury. The division of Wales into four territorially defined dioceses was itself an effect of Norman influence. There seems to have been no bishop at Llanelwy (St Asaph) before the first Norman appointment.[21] The early-twelfth-century bishop of Glamorgan, Urban, built a cathedral at Llandaff and struggled to secure a strong position within the Welsh Church by enlisting the support of Canterbury and Rome: he was the first bishop in Wales to profess obedience to Canterbury on his appointment in 1107. When St David's argued that she, not Canterbury, had metropolitan authority over the Welsh church, it was a Norman bishop of St David's, Bishop Bernard, who had turned St David's claim to pre-eminence into this practical claim to administrative power.

Within the dioceses, the Normans established the normal

machinery of church organization—territorial parishes, rural deaneries, and archdeaconries. Through these administrative channels, Canterbury—and ultimately Rome—was able to set about the gradual process of enforcing conformity to Roman usage in every detail of Welsh Christian life.

Yet it was to take many centuries for all the Welsh colouring of Christianity to fade. After the Welsh *clasau* were disbanded or reformed, and houses of the regular medieval religious orders were established, the Welsh recognized in the spirit of the Cistercians something akin to their own religious feeling. The Cistercian monasteries were swelled by Welsh recruits, and Strata Florida (in the lonely moorland south-east of Aberystwyth) proved especially instrumental in preserving Welsh traditions. The cults of the Welsh saints remained popular, despite competition from cults such as those of the Virgin and the Trinity popularized by the Normans in Wales. If the body of the Celtic Church in Wales was dead, something of its spirit was to persist.

2

The Christian Sites

In western Britain, life was not based in cities and towns and villages: the British freemen were primarily pastoralists, living in scattered homesteads (*trefi*). Bondsmen might be grouped in small settlements (*taeogdrefi*) where they worked their lords' lands. Dwellings were in general too flimsy to have left any recognizable trace: as late as the twelfth century, Giraldus Cambrensis in his *Itinerary of Wales* described the houses of the Welsh as built of woven osiers and lasting but a year.

Many of the sites chosen by the early Christians for their burial-grounds or churches or monasteries seem to us picturesquely isolated. Partrishow, in its beautiful valley setting in the heart of the Black Mountains; Penmon, where seagulls wheel above a church remote from the homes of modern men. But since concentrations of population are a recent development in Wales, the fact that an early Christian site may be isolated today tells us nothing about its original relationship to the settlement pattern. Sometimes by chance later developments have attracted settlers to a site that was once a lonely hermitage: populous Merthyr Tydfil was once a deserted wilderness chosen by anchorites for retreat.[1] Sometimes a site that was once a major religious centre is now relatively undeveloped, like the tiny cathedral city of St David's. As we shall see, many of the early Christian sites, for instance Llangadwaladr in Anglesey, were founded near the courts of princes, while others, such as Llantwit and St David's, were strategically placed in relation to sea- or land-routes. Lonely hermitages were by no means typical.[2]

Today the Church as an institution is strongly identified in our minds with the church as a building—the parish church with which we are so familiar. But it was the Normans who established the parochial system in Wales; and the church buildings as we know them are medieval or later in date (though many may stand on much earlier Christian sites, and just occasionally some early features are preserved in the later structures).

A clue to the character of the Celtic forerunners of these churches is given by the Welsh word for them, *llannau*. As any visitor to Wales immediately notices, the country suffers from a surfeit of place-names beginning with *llan*, often followed by the name of the saint to whom the church is dedicated. Llanddewi is the church of St David; Llanilltud, that of St Illtud. The name of the church has come to denote the settlement that has grown up around or near it. Originally, however, *llan* designated a religious enclosure. The earliest identifiable Christian sites in Celtic Britain are cemeteries, consecrated burial-grounds for converts.[3] The manner and place of burial were all-important for a faith which preached actual bodily resurrection. In Roman times, cemeteries—whether Christian or pagan—had been located outside settlements, to cope with the dead from the settlement and the surrounding district; large, usually unenclosed cemeteries of this type continued to be used in the fifth and sixth centuries. But these centuries also saw the appearance of a type of cemetery distinctive to Britain and Ireland, a small burial-ground enclosed by a circular (or at least curvilinear) earthwork or wall. These small cemeteries must have been intended for limited use— perhaps by a single kin-group. Presumably each would be founded by a cleric or by a group of monks for the burial of the community they served.

Buildings dedicated to religious use were less essential than cemeteries. The pagan Celts had worshipped in the open air, and the same would have been true of Christian converts, for several centuries at least. A portable or permanent cross might be set up to mark the spot where a cleric would preach, and there were portable altars for celebration of Mass. Rivers or wells were the most convenient places for baptism. Except for princes' households and other communities served by their own priest or bishop, most of the scattered populace would be dependent for ministry on occasional visits by clergy.

However, at the sites where the clergy were based, it would be convenient for them to have chapels or oratories for their own use. In Galloway, an important centre of early British Christianity, excavations on Ardwall Isle have revealed a sequence of development that was probably typical of early British Christian sites.[4] First, perhaps in the late fifth century, some Christian burials were made there; later, a small timber oratory was built within the cemetery, and further burials were made in alignment with this building; finally, perhaps in the early eighth century, the oratory was replaced by a chapel of stone. An oval bank surrounds the site: in its present form, the bank does not pre-date the timber oratory, but it could have replaced an earlier boundary.

Those churches standing today whose sites originated as early Christian burial-grounds can be recognized by the following features: their graveyards will be built up by layer upon layer of burials, and will be circular, or at least rounded in shape; early memorial-stones or stone crosses may have been found in the vicinity; and the churches will probably be dedicated to local, Welsh saints.[5] It is easiest to recognize these features at isolated country sites, free of interference from later settlement. At Mynydd Illtud, for example, on a high common facing the jagged peaks of the Brecon Beacons (near the new Mountain Centre), is a deserted and derelict church. The existing structure is of no great antiquity; but the dedication to the native St Illtud argues for early foundation of the site. Sheep now roam over the tumbled tombstones within the circular churchyard, which is enclosed by a bank. This seems a good candidate for a Christian site dating back to the days of the Celtic church—although usually the Christian founders preferred sites in valleys or on the spurs of hills. Many early Christian sites must remain unidentified: indeed, many will have been abandoned in the 1,500 years or so since their foundation, and unless chance excavation unearths their graves, they are unlikely to be recognized. Even from recent centuries we have numerous chance references to chapels and churches of which no vestige now remains.[6]

It is possible that some at least of the sites granted for Christian use had formerly had pagan associations. To redirect former religious activity into the new Christian channels made obvious good sense: St Augustine's mission to the Anglo-Saxons was instructed by Pope Gregory that wherever possible old temples should be converted and pagan traditions Christianized. The resultant continuity would make it easier for people to accept the new faith. A pagan burial-place, for instance, could easily be taken over as a Christian cemetery. A North British example of this is the cemetery on St Ninian's Isle, Bute, where a group of 'long cist' graves (graves, lined with stone slabs, long enough to accommodate a stretched-out body) was later partially enclosed by a circular stone-and-turf wall, within which similar burials were made. These later burials, however, were almost all oriented, that is, lying east-west, a Christian practice. Long cist graves have been discovered at several Christian sites in Wales, including Clynnog Fawr and Ynys Seiriol. Even if these are all Christian burials, and do not represent the Christian use of pagan sites, they at least illustrate the readiness of the Christians to employ what had been a pagan form of burial.[7]

Water, essential as it is to life, was certainly involved in pagan ceremonies in Britain, as throughout the world. Spectacular evidence is the hoard of bronze and iron goods recovered from Llyn Cerrig Bach in Anglesey; apparently these objects were cast into the lake as offerings in the centuries immediately preceding the Roman occupation. Many of what came to be regarded by Christians as holy wells may originally have been the scenes of pagan rites. Often these wells are nothing more imposing than tiny springs of water bubbling from the ground. Almost every church in Wales today can boast its holy well near by, though patient hunting through the long grass of a neglected churchyard may be needed to locate it.

Monks and clerics and anchorites would naturally choose to settle where fresh water was to hand.[8] Presumably, if a spring could be found with sacred associations, so much the better—the Christian settlement would have a flying start in gaining the local population's esteem. Later, it was claimed that the wells' special powers were derived from their links with the local saints, the reputed founders of the sites. This proved so useful a means of enhancing a saint's reputation and attracting revenue to his foundations that the *Lives* of the Welsh saints are peppered with stories about the miraculous origins and powers of the saints' wells.

Even the form taken by the Celtic Christian sites was influenced by pre-Christian custom. Very occasionally, an early monastic site in Britain or Ireland is surrounded by a rectangular earthwork (as at Iona and Clonmacnois), probably in imitation of the rectangular ramparts with which the monasteries in the deserts of Egypt, Palestine, and Asia Minor protected themselves from human and animal marauders. But the formal layout of settlements on a rectangular plan, though introduced to Britain by the Romans, was alien to British tradition. The British strongholds were hill or promontory forts, where curvilinear defences were required by the contours of the ground; circular defences were also used on flatter ground, for instance for the small defended homesteads or raths[9] common in Dyfed.[10] Pagan religious sites had taken the same form, such as Cold Kitchen Hill in Wiltshire, which is simply an area of ground demarcated by an insubstantial earthwork. In ringing their sites by earthworks, the Christians were employing a form that already had a religious as well as a secular connotation in Britain.

The bank-and-ditch, or hedge, or wall enclosing a Christian foundation fulfilled a variety of purposes. It showed that the site was set aside for a special purpose—an important function since, apart from this boundary, only a tiny oratory and perhaps a monument or two might mark the smaller Christian foundations. It kept grazing animals out, except presumably those of the clerics or monks, without whose help the enclosures would have become impossibly overgrown. It defined the limits of consecrated ground, and controlled human access to the site. Within the enclosure, the church gave sanctuary to fugitives, in accordance with the Old Testament instruction: 'Ye shall appoint . . . cities of refuge . . . that the slayer may flee thither.'[11] Few earthworks would have been substantial enough to repel attack: even the massive ramparts of hill forts needed to be lined with warriors when under siege. The church employed more subtle means to protect its foundations: it impressed the populace with the sanctity of the enclosed ground, and exacted compensation for any violations that did occur. Hence the churches' vulnerability when enemies arrived—notably the Vikings—who had no fear of the Christian God.

The simple buildings which were built within the enclosures ranged from a single oratory to monasteries the size of villages; these buildings, like the enclosures, followed native models. The normal materials currently used for building in Wales were turf, wattle-and-daub, timber, and thatch. In the rest of Britain, stone was generally used where available; but as Aileen Fox has commented: 'It is a strange fact . . . that whereas stone for building is abundant in most districts in Wales, stone huts of any period are limited in distribution, occurring chiefly in Anglesey, Caernarvonshire and Merioneth, and in Pembrokeshire.'[12] Since the remains of the less durable structures are hard to detect, most of our evidence for British buildings comes from the stone-using areas. Two types of dwelling have been recognized on post-Roman sites: the circular hut (popular since the Bronze Age), and the rectilinear hut, and both have been found on early Christian sites. It used to be thought that the rectilinear plan, with the improved roofing techniques it required, was borrowed from Roman architecture; but the design may have developed independently in pre-Roman Britain.[13]

The best and earliest example so far discovered in western Britain of an early Celtic monastic site is Tintagel, in Cornwall. The buildings there are more or less rectangular, which may well be a reflection of the Mediterranean influence to which monasticism itself was indebted (though it could also be explained by an already-established tradition of building rectilinear huts). As in the early monastic settlements in the East, there were individual cells for the monks; it seems that, like the early desert monks before them, they would have spent much of their time alone, but there were a few larger buildings at Tintagel, presumably intended for communal use. There were also a few larger buildings for the few communal activities, some outhouses and store-rooms, a burial-ground, and an oratory. The whole settlement was enclosed by a bank and ditch which cut off the promontory on which it stood.

Archaeologists have yet to uncover as rewarding a site in Wales. Often, later building will have obliterated the earlier structures. At Clynnog Fawr, on the north shore of the Lleyn Peninsula, the remains of a small rectangular building have been found beneath the sixteenth-century chapel known as Eglwys y Bedd.[14] Clynnog Fawr was the centre of the cult of St Beuno, the most influential of the north Welsh saints. A fine church of late Perpendicular style stands there now; from beneath the tower a narrow, vaulted stone passage leads to Eglwys y Bedd, where the outline of the earlier building is marked by bluish stones inserted in the floor.[15] A row of thirteen burials was found beyond the east end of the building. It seems that the structure of Eglwys y Bedd deliberately enclosed an earlier chapel. Presumably this earlier building was the former church of St Beuno, from which the relics of the saint were translated to the new tomb provided for them in Eglwys y Bedd. Unfortunately the date of the earlier building is uncertain. It was prudent to build in durable stone after the Viking firebrands sent so many timber churches up in flames; this church could conceivably date from the rebuilding at Clynnog following the devastating Viking raid in A.D. 978. On the other hand, in Ireland building in stone seems to have come into fashion in the twelfth century, and the early stone church at Clynnog may be representative of a similarly timed change in fashion in Wales. Or it could represent a still later phase in the site's history. We simply do not know.

Not far away, on the south-east tip of Anglesey, was another influential religious centre, connected with St Seiriol. There were two separate but related foundations: Penmon, on the mainland of Anglesey, and Ynys Seiriol, an island half a mile offshore.[16] On Ynys Seiriol, the remains of three or four rectangular stone cells underlie early medieval buildings. They are enclosed by a roughly oval wall; and traces of an early field system are associated with the settlement. These remains do not necessarily date back as far as the earliest Christian settlement on the island: throughout the life of the Celtic church the smaller, self-sufficient communities of monks or anchorites would have followed the same plan. An oratory would probably have stood at the centre of the enclosure on Ynys Seiriol, where later church buildings now stand. Adjoining the ruined twelfth-century church tower is a tiny stone chapel no more than five feet square: it is thought to be of eleventh-century date, but it serves as a reminder of the minute size of the pre-medieval churches in Celtic Britain. The church building, however sacred, was not the predominant feature of a Christian site, as it is today.

At Penmon, a splendid Norman church was erected in the eleventh century, with a carved tympanum over the doorway: a rare feature is the survival of the original stone-roofing of its tower. Of earlier churches on the site—of the church burnt by the Vikings in A.D. 971 and of the structure presumably built to replace it—as usual we have no trace. However, behind the church (reached by a path leading off to the left opposite the stone dovecote beyond the churchyard) are early structures grouped around St Seiriol's well. The well, springing up at the foot of a little inland cliff, is encased in a probably eighteenth-century shelter; but in front of it, nestled against the wall of the cliff, is a ring of massive boulders, the base of a circular stone hut, just large enough for a person to lie down in. Local tradition identifies this as St Seiriol's cell. While this can never be proved, it is perfectly feasible. Many of the Welsh monasteries would have originated, as later traditions claimed, as the settlements of individual hermits like Seiriol, with perhaps a follower or two: their dedication would attract followers, until eventually a size-able religious community would be established on the site, from which individuals might set out to found new hermitages or monasteries.

The meagre and unimpressive remains on sites such as Ynys Seiriol and Penmon give us little idea of the former splendour and liveliness of the major religious establishments. As we shall see in Chapter 6, inscribed and carved stone monuments and the rare survivals of manuscripts and literary works give us a better impression of the quality of the monks' and clerics' lives. In their prime, the great Welsh foundations were full of bustle and activity; they were perhaps the largest settlements known among the British, 'cities' on the model of those prescribed for the priests and Levites in Old Testament legislation.[17] As a community grew in size and acquired more and more land to support itself, it became involved in all the tasks that face a large land-owner: the management of tenants, the collection, storage, and preparation of food and fuel and other necessities; and the education of children—whether tenants' children, or those dedicated

29

by their parents to the religious life, or children sent boarding-school fashion for training, or sometimes the children of the ecclesiastics themselves.[18] A guest-house would be needed for visitors, who might range from the local prince to a visiting Irish abbot. If the community were the guardians of a revered shrine or well—and in the later days of the Celtic church most of them saw to it that they were—they would have to deal not only with a steady flow of donations, but with an accompanying flow of pilgrims, all of whom would have to be welcomed, ministered to, and fed.

Some monastic sites seem to have been deliberately chosen for their accessibility to visitors and travellers. Llanilltud (now Llantwit Major) and Llancarfan,[19] the major foundations in Glamorgan before Llandaff rose to prominence, had access to the coast at points affording an easy crossing of the Bristol Channel, while just inland passed the major Roman road across the South Wales coastal plain, a route which was almost certainly still in use.[20] In these monasteries, the busy life of a port must have been added to agricultural concerns; and traders and pilgrims from south-west Britain or further afield must have mingled with the monks and the tenants of their estates, the guests, children, servants, and workmen, who would each have been pursuing their business within the confines of the monastery. How large the religious settlements could be has been demonstrated by air photography at Llanafanfawr, in Breconshire, where the church and cemetery are contained within a circular enclosure four hundred feet in diameter.

One can sympathize with the desire of some devout Christians to escape from the inevitably worldly concerns of such centres. From the beginning, there was a strong tendency towards eremeticism in the Celtic church. It was the retreat of hermits to the deserts of the Eastern Mediterranean lands that had inspired the development of monasticism, and when monasticism spread to Britain it brought with it the idea that the ultimate in religious life was complete withdrawal from the world. The British had no deserts to retreat to: they had to find alternative wildernesses—impenetrable wooded valleys, hillside caves, or storm-swept, rocky islets. The word *Merthyr* in Welsh place-names such as

Merthyr Tydfil derives from Latin *martyrium*, but it has nothing to do with martyrdom in the sense of one killed for his faith (whatever local traditions may say!); it was those who sought a more prolonged form of sacrifice that are thus remembered, for *martyrium* could also mean 'a monastic retreat'.

Perhaps it is the remote coastal or island hermitages—such as tiny St Tudwal's Island East, off the south coast of the Lleyn Peninsula—whose asperity is most readily sensed by us today. But not all coastal sites would have been austere. A fertile island or coastal valley, with some shelter, and access to a plentiful supply of fish, would have offered an easier life than many inland sites; and at a time when communication by sea was easier than overland, it would have been by no means isolated. From prehistoric times people had chosen—without any desire to mortify themselves—to live on the edges of the sea, where the cliffs provided protection from enemies. Caldey Island was the home of one of the earliest monasteries in Wales; today, it still houses a monastery, and provides homes for laymen, too. The gentler slopes are farmed, and from the luxuriant growth of wild plants the monks extract scent which they use in the production of toiletries. The island is easily accessible, and boatloads of tourists make the half-mile crossing from the mainland. Until the black specks of the Viking boats were spotted on the horizon, the more favourable coastal sites must have been pleasant places to live.

Inland, the church founders normally chose valley sites: these too ranged from the harsh to the comfortable. The *Life of St Cadog* says that the saint heard 'that about the river Neath there were many places solitary and suitable for hermits' (para. 20), and it is of course in the mining valleys of South Wales that several *Merthyr* place-names bear witness to early hermitages. These steep-sided valleys were densely wooded before they were denuded for industrial purposes. Occasionally, in their upper reaches, the woods survive: around Ystradfellte, for instance, deep tree-hung gorges reverberate with the sound of waterfalls, and are lonely and rather frightening places, even today. Wild animals, and sometimes outlaws, lurked in the woods. But worst of all were the supernatural terrors. St Brynach's biographer tells us that when the saint settled at the site now called Pontfaen in

31

the Gwaun Valley (in north Pembrokeshire), 'he freed that place from unclean spirits. They, roving about it every night with dreadful outcries, and filling it with horrid howlings, rendered it uninhabitable till that day' (para. 5). The writer was not only making for Brynach a claim made for countless other saints; he was effectively stressing what an eerie spot the saint had chosen. At night, these woods would be full of strange sounds: the scream of a vixen, a hedgehog's heavy breathing, the sudden scuffle of mice in the undergrowth.

Broader, more open valleys could be extremely favourable places to settle. Llanilltud (Llantwit) in the fertile basin of the river Ogney is a good example, and St Illtud's biographer paints a glowing picture of the site's merits. ' "Appoint husbandmen over this territory" ', the site's donor, king Meirchion, tells the saint, ' "for this territory is meet to be cultivated, and there is none more fertile throughout the country. Tilled, it abounds in harvests; it is seen to be flowing with honey and fragrant with flowers. Italy is fertile . . . this is more abundant and more temperate . . . Too much cold does not destroy the crops, superfluous heat does not parch the fruits." ' (*Life of St Illtud*, para. 10.)

The character of a site can be a valuable clue to its founder's intentions, but the way the site was developed was not dependent on geography alone. There was a tradition of asceticism at St David's, but this does not seem to have been related to any unusual remoteness or harshness in the site. Like the great monasteries of Glamorgan, St David's was well placed in relation to land- and sea-routes, being hidden from the eyes of sea-raiders, yet having easy access to the coast. Intercourse with Ireland was especially close and fruitful. Rhigyfarch, St David's biographer, describes the site as a 'pleasant spot' (ch. 3), where St Patrick would have liked to settle, had not God had other plans for him.

The Welsh saints are commonly believed to have founded the churches which are dedicated to them. It was a peculiarly Celtic custom to dedicate churches to their founders. Perhaps at first a religious site was simply called by the founder's name, just as the meeting-places of the early Christians in the Roman Empire had been known by the names of the houses' owners. However, from the fifth century onwards it became popular on the Continent to dedicate churches to saints and martyrs, especially those whose relics the churches possessed. Presumably it was in response to this development that the Celtic Christians eventually turned their own site-names into formal church dedications for the oratories or churches that had been built on the sites.[21] If the founder of the site was unknown, or if the cult of another saint had become more influential in the area, an alternative saint would be honoured in the dedication.

Their role as founders has ensured that the names of the saints have survived from an age when most persons and events slipped away unremembered. Unfortunately, we have very little authentic information about these saints. Their names are usually found in Wales in the Brittonic form, that is, in the branch of the Celtic language that was spoken in Celtic mainland Britain and in its offshoot, Brittany. The name of St Illtud's chief foundation, modern Llantwit (from *Llanyltwyt*), is unusual in that it derives from the Goidelic, or Irish, form of the saint's name:[22] the Brittonic form was Eltut, as preserved in the place-name Llanelltud, in Merionethshire. Brittonic evolved into something resembling modern Welsh in the sixth century, and as contact declined between the Brittonic-speaking areas, divergence produced the three languages—Welsh, Cornish, and Breton—still, to varying degrees, in use today. When the same saint was known in different areas of the Celtic lands, his name might acquire variant local forms: St Cybi, commemorated at Caergybi (Holyhead), appears as Cuby in a Cornish place-name; the Irish St Aidan of Ferns is probably identifiable with the Madog celebrated at Llanmadog and Capel Madog in Wales (from the derivative form of the name, Mo-aid-og). Among educated circles, and in written records, the saints' names were known in Latinized form: Dubricius for St Dyfrig; Paternus for St Padarn. With all this variation, it is easy to see why confusion arose. Sometimes collectors of traditions about the early saints seem to have confused two or more saints with similar names. Paternus was a popular name in Roman and sub-Roman times, and it seems that the author of the *Life of St Padarn* mistakenly identified the

33

Welsh saint with one or more saints of the same name remembered in Brittany.[23]

Most of the saints commemorated in Wales have also left their mark—either personally, or through their followers—elsewhere in the Celtic lands. Unless, like David, Illtud, Samson, etc., they are connected by early traditions with the area that is now Wales, it is hard to tell where these saints originated or were most active. The saints' *Lives* purport to describe the travels of the saints between their foundations, both within Welsh territory and further afield. St Cybi is said to have been born and brought up in Cornwall, and only to have come to Wales after a visit to Jerusalem and a fifty-year sojourn with St Hilary of Poitiers. Even then he interrupted his stay in Wales for a lengthy visit to Ireland. It is tempting to accept such accounts as explanations for the distribution of dedications to a saint; but we must remember that in almost every case the hagiographers were, like us, dealing with events centuries before their own time. Like us, they had the evidence of the distribution of a saint's cult to guide them, and, like us, they were anxious to make sense of this evidence. Rarely can we believe that their version of the saint's travels is any more than conjecture, conveniently shaped to suit the best interests of the foundations with which the hagiographer himself was connected.[24]

The modern scholar must be more critical. Where the dedications are of value is in showing us the extent of the different cults, and suggesting the most likely routes by which they were spread. Taking St Cybi again as an example, his dedications in Wales are all on or near to the coast. Apart from Caergybi (Holyhead), he is remembered at Llangybi (near Pwllheli); at another Llangybi, in the Teifi valley; in the island name, Ynys Gybi, off the north coast of Pembrokeshire; and at Llangibby-on-Usk in Gwent. Diffusion of his cult by the coastal sea-routes seems the only possible explanation.

The distribution of dedications cannot, as the hagiographers assumed, reveal the movements of the saint himself. They represent the influence of a cult after many centuries during which the relative prestige of the various saints must have undergone often profound changes. Surviving dedications to St Padarn are surprisingly few—seven are noted by Bowen[25]—in view of

34

the early importance of his chief foundation, Llanbadarn Fawr; while dedications to St David are scattered so thickly in South Wales that the saint would have been far from the withdrawn ascetic of tradition had he personally founded all these sites. As a saint's cult grew in popularity, and his foundations grew in power, more and more churches would be founded in, or re-dedicated to, his name. Unfortunately, it is impossible to trace the history of all but a handful of the church dedications in Wales back into pre-Norman times. But we know that under Norman influence the pattern of dedications in Wales was radically changed. A flood of dedications and re-dedications to non-Celtic figures—biblical saints and members of the Holy Family—left Celtic dedications in relatively short supply in the thoroughly Normanized borderlands and south-east coastal plain.[26] More recently, many dedications to Celtic saints have been forgotten simply because the sites so dedicated have fallen into disuse.

Long after the true facts of a saint's career were forgotten, all sorts of traditions might develop to explain his connection with the areas where his name was remembered. We can no more assume that the saints visited all the wells and chapels named after them than we can believe that Arthur visited every 'Arthur's seat' and 'Arthur's quoit'. And just as Arthurian tradition became localized in all parts of Britain—in each of the areas that are now Wales and Cornwall and Brittany—so the traditions of the saints could have been transplanted to areas which they themselves had never visited. The overseas connections of their subjects proved convenient for the twelfth-century hagiographers, who could compensate for the sparsity of Welsh traditions about some saints by padding out their *Lives* with traditions borrowed from else-where. Of twenty paragraphs into which the *Life of St Cybi* is divided, only eight and a half concern events in Wales. Western Britain was not yet split up into Strathclyde and Wales and Cornwall at the time when the saints were active, and since cultural contact was close between all the Celtic lands fronting the Irish Sea, there is every reason to suppose that the saints did travel widely (like some of their better-documented Irish counter-parts). The early *Life of St Samson* traces his journey from South Wales, via the south-west peninsula of Britain, to settle in

35

Brittany. But normally, tracing the footsteps of the saints can be little more than guesswork.

More reliable than dedications as evidence for the early centres of Christianity in Wales are the inscribed stones or slabs which the early British Christians erected to commemorate their dead. About 139 of these simple monuments survive. Although only a handful are dated—even approximately—by their inscriptions, on stylistic grounds they are believed to date from the fifth to the seventh centuries, the time when the saints were active.[27] The custom of erecting inscribed memorials or tombstones was derived ultimately from pagan Roman practice; but the style of the British inscriptions and their predominantly coastal distribution along the western shores of Britain argue that the erectors of these monuments were not copying the tombstones of Roman Britain, but were following a fashion re-imported, in a Christian context, from Gaul, with which, as we have seen, Britain was in trade contact at this time. Within the area that is now Wales, it is the north-west and south-west peninsulas, most accessible from the sea-routes, that boast the heaviest concentrations of inscribed stones.

The monuments are exciting evidence, for through the words of the inscriptions the early British Christians speak directly to us. Usually, the inscriptions tell us only the name of the commemorated person, but occasionally we learn more. A sixth-century monument from Margam Mountain proudly goes into details about the dead man's ancestry: '[The stone] of Bodvoc. Here he lies, son of Catotigirnus (and) great-grandson of Eternalis Vedomavus.'[28] Indications of the commemorated person's descent were generally avoided on Christian memorial stones of this period, perhaps in obedience to the biblical instruction 'Call no man your father upon the earth, for one is your Father, which is in heaven.'[29] But one can imagine how the British chieftains, accustomed to having their genealogies recited in their honour, would have been unable to resist the opportunity of recording their ancestry in a form whose permanence no oral culture could match.

There is a concentration of monuments with unusually detailed inscriptions in Gwynedd, showing that that area was an important focus of early Christian activity. At Llansadwrn, Anglesey,[30] a memorial inscription commemorates the site's founder, 'blessed Saturninus'. Here we have firm proof that the saint was associated in person with the site that took his name. Evangelists from Gaul may have helped to establish the church in western Britain, but the monuments show that this is only part of the story. Some monuments bear inscriptions in Irish in the Ogam script; some use forms of wording borrowed from fashions current in North Africa. Like the imported pottery, the monuments show that in the formative years of the Celtic church, in the centuries when Gildas's clergy were kowtowing to the local princes, and when the saints were settling in the valleys and coastlands of Wales to devote themselves to the service of God, a whole range of foreign influences were at work in western Britain, shaping the development of the Church. Once the initial conversion-work had been accomplished by evangelists from overseas, native clergy would have been trained and ordained to carry on the work—as we know happened in the better-recorded conversions of the Irish and the Anglo-Saxons; but these native clergy would continue to be responsive to the ideas that filtered through from the church both in Gaul and in more distant lands.

Christianity was not necessarily strongest in the areas where the monuments are most numerous. South-east Wales seems to have been an early centre of Christian activity, but has few monuments—probably because here Christianity was carried over from Roman times, whereas the fashion of erecting monuments was re-introduced into Britain after the end of the Roman occupation by evangelists who sought to convert areas still pagan in belief. Moreover, it is perhaps a trifle suspicious that the distribution of the stone monuments coincides with that of stone buildings: elsewhere monuments, like buildings, could have been made of wood. The Ogam alphabet was probably devised for use on wood; and when the British came to carve crosses on their monuments, their designs sometimes seem to be based on wooden crosses. Wood was possibly used, too, for simple grave-markers, for people not important enough to merit an elaborate monument. As Charles Thomas has suggested,[31] it is hard to see how the Christians could have arranged their burials in the regular parallel rows found in early cemeteries, unless some form of marker was used.

It is clear that, although the Celtic church in Britain went through periods of comparative isolation, there was a great deal of travelling by the Welsh saints and their successors, both within the area that is now Wales and further afield. Travel in Celtic Britain was an exciting challenge for those of an adventurous spirit. To be able to travel at all was a rare privilege. In a self-sufficient society, one's home was one's source of food and clothing and fuel. Moreover, people viewed strangers with suspicion, for why should men with nothing to hide choose to leave their homes and kinsfolk? In Celtic society, one privileged class of people had managed to overcome these restrictions on movement: they were the professional men of the arts—bards, prophets, druids. Their professional skills ensured them a welcome at the princes' courts, where all their needs would be supplied. Poems convincingly credited to the early British poet, Taliesin, are dedicated to rulers of kingdoms as far apart as Powys and Rheged (a North British kingdom in the Carlisle area). The Christian priests and monks who took over from the druids as religious specialists were able to inherit their mobility. As Christians, their dependence on lay patronage may have been a disadvantage in that it left them less free to criticize their patrons, and thus produced the obsequiousness that Gildas condemns; but without this patronage they would have had no freedom of movement. An inscribed stone at Llanelhaiarn in Caernarvonshire[32] commemorates a stranger from Elmet (a North British kingdom in the area of Leeds) who was perhaps an itinerant British evangelist. As monks and clerics grew in numbers and in wealth, they were able to provide their travelling colleagues with hospitality.

Travel by sea proved attractive in an age before man had achieved much in the way of conquering the innumerable obstacles that impeded progress by land—especially in mountainous regions like Wales: forests, unfordable rivers, marshes, hostile tribes. Yet looking out across the Irish sea from the Welsh coast on a grey and windswept day, one can feel only admiration for the courage of the early sailors. The standard Celtic boat was a wicker-framed vessel covered with cow-hide—rather like the surviving Welsh coracle, but different in shape. The long, narrow Irish curraghs, which still set out to sea, laden sometimes with cattle or sheep as well as their human cargo, are a closer parallel.[33] A continuous tradition of skin boats of this type can be traced back in Britain as far as the Bronze Age: they were nowhere near as delicate as they look, for, quoting E. G. Bowen, the 'fine curved sheer and long lifting bows ... enable them to rise and ride over almost any sea. With a good following wind it has been estimated that they can accomplish as much as ninety miles in a day.'[34] Besides, these boats had great advantages when land was reached, for the sailors did not have to look out for sheltered harbours: they could simply carry their boats up on to the shore. When the treacherous currents made it dangerous to sail around headlands, the light skin boats could be beached and carried across the headland, and the voyage continued from the further shore. The distribution of saints' cults indicates that churchmen travelling from what is now Wales to Brittany avoided Land's End by crossing central Cornwall.

The foreign trading vessels which brought their cargoes of pottery, oil, and wine to the British coast would have been built of timber, and occasionally we hear of the Celts using timber boats. In the twelfth century, the author of the *Life of St Tatheus* cannot have had a skin boat in mind when he wrote of the boat in which the saint had sailed to Gwent from Ireland needing to be moored (paras. 3–4). What looks like a carving of a boat, on an eleventh- or twelfth-century grave slab at Llanfaglan, Caernarvonshire,[35] appears to be built of planks, and has a mast.[36]

Navigation, without modern aids, would have presented many problems. But the Celts were dauntless: sometimes penitents or those wishing to make an extreme sacrifice for God set to sea at God's mercy, in a boat without rudder or oars. Tatheus and his companions were alleged to have crossed from Ireland in this manner, travelling 'without rower and sail and oar, wherever the blowing of the winds directed them' (para. 3). More conventional navigators on the Irish sea-routes had one important advantage: on days of good visibility, they could before departure catch a glimpse of their ultimate goal. For instance, St Cybi and his successors at Caergybi could, from the top of Holyhead Mountain, have sighted not only the Welsh mountains of the mainland, and the North British mountains of modern Cumberland, but peaks on the Isle of Man and in distant Ireland.

The *Life of St Samson* gives two days as the time it took the saint to reach Caldey Island from Dun Etair (near Dublin). On such long voyages, unseen storms and navigational errors must have wrecked many a craft. But the turbulent straits between islands and the mainland could make short crossings equally perilous. We are told that St Cadog, with somewhat unchristian maliciousness, sent two of his disciples to row back from Barry Island to the nearby island of Echni (modern Flat Holm) to recover a manuscript they had forgotten. The hagiographer visualizes Cadog 'Sitting on the top of a hill' to watch them: 'in mid-ocean, the boat being unexpectedly overturned, they were drowned.' (*Life of St Cadog*, para. 29.)[37] The Welsh name for Bardsey (one of the most important pilgrimage centres in early Wales) is Ynys Enlli, which has been interpreted as meaning 'Island of the tides'. This would be an appropriate designation, for so hazardous is the crossing that even with modern boats the crossing may be impossible in bad weather for a week or more at a time.

Safely arrived travellers had good reason to give thanks to God. Many of the tiny chapels and hermitages dotted around the shores of the Celtic lands, whatever the purpose for which they were founded, came to serve as praying-stations for departing and returning travellers. Pilgrims to the great shrines would first be welcomed at these chapels. For instance, St David's was surrounded by chapels, situated in the coves where the pilgrims would land—St Justinian, St Non's, the chapel of St Patrick at Porth Mawr (Whitesands), and so on, 'All . . . near ye sea side, being there placed to draw ye devotion of ye seamen and passengers when they first came ashore.'[38]

The land of Wales has always tended to be split into two distinctive cultural areas, the North and the South, by the mountains at its core. To some extent, use of the sea-routes overcame this barrier: some saints' cults, such as that of Cybi, spread to both areas by inshore routes. However, on the whole, sea-travel encouraged the division: the south coast looked across the Bristol Channel to the south-west peninsula, and ultimately to Brittany; the north coast looked across Morecambe Bay to the North British lands. These different contacts made the Christian culture of North Wales quite distinct from that of the South. In the North, many of the local saints were claimed—doubtless after their true parentage had been forgotten—to be descendants of the North British prince, Cunedda, who was believed to have come to Wales to drive out the Irish settlers. Other saints were said to be descendants of Coel Godebog, the North British ruler immortalized as King Cole. In South Wales, there was a similar grouping of saints, this time fathered on Brychan, supposed founder of the kingdom of Brycheiniog (modern Breconshire). How much credence should be given to such claims is indicated by the fact that in Cornwall an entirely different list of saints were claimed as Brychan's children.

Welsh traditions and folklore borrowed heavily from North Britain, so it is not surprising that the cult of St Kentigern of Strathclyde found a foothold in North Wales.[39] Interestingly, we have some evidence too of influence travelling from Wales to Strathclyde, for a Welsh saint, Cadog, had a church dedicated to him at Cambuslang on the Clyde.

For travel inland, the remains of the Roman roads would have provided the most direct and easily followed routes. Since there had been little civil settlement in western highland Britain, the road network had never been extensive: the Romans had needed roads mainly for the transport of troops, or for access to mines. But it was by what roads there were that the cults of the saints and the fashion of erecting stone monuments spread inland.[40] Like most Roman products, the roads had been made to last. Usually the surface was metalled; the roads were flanked by ditches for drainage, and they pressed straight on to their destination, overcoming natural obstacles with stout bridges and causeways. Even when the use-furrowed surface had been choked by vegetation, and the bridges had collapsed or been swept away by floods, travellers would find it easier to stick as closely as they could to the course of the roads than to strike out without guidance (except from a few less-direct native tracks) across country.

Occasionally, the early British Christians set up monuments to their dead alongside the Roman roads. High on the moors above Ystradfellte one can still walk along the broad track, known as Sarn Helen, that was once the Roman road from the fort at Brecon (Y Gaer) to the coast at Neath. Beside the track, visible from afar across the undulating moorland, towers a great finger of stone, Maen Madoc (the stone of Madoc).[41] An inscription on its side declares that 'Dervacus son of Justus lies here.' Perhaps influenced by the Roman custom of roadside burial, Dervacus' commemorators were ensuring that his name would remain fresh in the memory of generations of passers-by.[42] Not far away, near Port Talbot, a Roman milestone has been discovered, which the Christians converted into a memorial stone.[43] An inscription was added on the back: 'Here lies Cantusus, his father was Paulinus', and the stone was reset upside down with its former inscription hidden.

Expediency governed the use by the British Christians of Roman remains; and this applied not only to roads and monuments. The founders of Christian sites were quite prepared to take advantage of the shelter and protection afforded by the now deserted Roman forts and settlements. At Caergybi, St Cybi's church stands within the massive ramparts of the Roman fort, built for defence against Irish sea-raiders in the later years of Roman rule. Tradition asserts that it was the infamous Maelgwn, sixth-century king of Gwynedd, who gave this site to St Cybi. The fort would have been out of use for approaching 200 years—years the stout walls could weather, but which would have seen the decay of the timber buildings within. In adopting such a site, the British Christians were not trying to return to a Roman way of life; the Irish, who had never experienced Roman occupation, were equally ready to avail themselves of the protection of Roman sites when they chose to settle in Britain. The Irish St Fursey founded a monastery in East Anglia within the great Roman fortress, Burgh Castle. The shells of Roman forts provided the Christians with boundaries for their religious enclosures far grander than any they could have constructed themselves.

In south-east Wales, three of St Samson's companions are said to have settled in a deserted fort, 'a very delightful castle', when Samson retreated to a cave in the Severn valley to live a hermit's life.[44] At Caerwent, the only major Roman civil settlement within the bounds of modern Wales, finds of coins attest some form of continued occupation into post-Roman times; but the settlement had become a shanty town, rather than a centre of civic pride. The *basilica* (the assembly-hall and council offices) had been destroyed by fire; houses were semi-ruinous. One can understand Gildas's lament that the cities of Britain lay neglected, deserted, and dismantled. When we find at Caerwent the remains of a small Christian church of post-Roman date, built not only after the main buildings on the site were in ruins, but with its foundations in a layer of debris one foot thick, it is impossible to believe that when the church was built the town's population were anything more than squatters—refugees, perhaps, from Saxon encroachment further to the east. They may have come from places where the Roman lifestyle had in some measure been preserved: the crumbling remains of a Roman town would have been the nearest they could get to the orderly urban existence which for them had become synonymous with civilization. St Tatheus, from Ireland, was reputed to have founded a church at Caerwent; but the account given in his twelfth-century *Life* (para. 6) is full of late and unauthentic details.[45] The church excavated at Caerwent is Byzantine in type, built on the basilican plan, and therefore seems far more likely to have been built by Christians from the Romanized areas of Britain. A similar church has been discovered at Winchester.

The Celtic Christians seem to have followed a special procedure when consecrating a site to the Lord. The English historian, Bede, writing in the early eighth century, described how St Cedd, a Northumbrian educated by the Irish monks at Lindisfarne, founded the Mercian monastery of Lastingham: Cedd first observed Lent with strict fasting on the site, for 'this, he said, was the custom of those of whom he had learned the rule of regular discipline: first to consecrate to our Lord, by prayer and fasting, the place which they had newly received for building a monastery or a church.'[46] This custom apparently underlies the statement in St Cybi's *Life* that on his arrival in southern Meath (in Ireland) 'he tarried forty days and so many nights. He built also in that place a church...' (para. 13).

3

Church Organization

We know from Gildas that the familiar Church officials (bishops, priests, and deacons) ran the affairs of the Church established in western Britain. What we do not know is how their responsibilities were defined. As we learn from the New Testament, the primitive Church had found it necessary to appoint leaders from each congregation to cope with administrative problems: as time went by, these officials came to be organized in a hierarchy modelled on that by which the civil provinces of the Roman Empire were administered. Bishops were installed in the provincial capitals, and governed territorial dioceses whose bounds coincided with those of the civil provinces. This system had been introduced into Gaul by late Roman times, and it may also have applied to the Romano-British Church across the Channel.

In western Britain, the framework of an urban-based civil administration was lacking, yet nevertheless it seems likely that when Christianity was gaining strength in the area in post-Roman times, its organization was diocesan. Gildas refers to the British clergy administering *paruchiae* (parishes), though he gives no indication as to how these were defined. The natural unit in Celtic society to which a bishop could attach himself would be the native kingdom or tribe.

There are some hints that one of the Welsh saints, Dyfrig (Dubricius) was the bishop of a territorial diocese, which had perhaps survived from Romano-British times. The *Life of St Samson*—an unusually early source—identifies him as a *papa* or *episcopus* (bishop); and the dedications to him occur in a tight cluster in the mid-Wye valley, in what was once the British kingdom of Erging. Dyfrig's chief foundation, at modern Hentland (from Welsh *Henllan*), was not far from Ariconium, the Roman town from which Erging took its name.[1] If the Church in lowland Britain was organized in territorial dioceses, as seems probable, it is only to be expected that the system would have extended into this area (to the south-east of what is now Wales), which was under civil government, like the lands further east. Interestingly, Dyfrig is traditionally the founding father of Welsh Christianity, while early Christian stone monuments are almost wholly absent from the area where his dedications are found:[2] perhaps the contact with Gaul which nourished the post-Roman development of the Church elsewhere in western Britain was less strongly felt here, where Christianity was already well established.

The provincial Roman bishops had, like secular administrators, become wealthy and influential figures. The British clergy in the highland regions, however less cultured, certainly possessed their share of self-importance, as the writings of St Patrick demonstrate.[3] St Patrick came from a family of Church officials, probably in north-west Britain. He was the grandson of a presbyter (priest) and son of a deacon. He in turn became a deacon, and eventually a bishop. But controversy surrounded his appointment as bishop; indeed, controversy seems to have beset his whole career, and his *Confession* reads as a defence by Patrick of his conduct, especially of the motives and methods of his mission-work in Ireland. It is obvious that at home Patrick had been bitterly attacked by the local church authorities, and the nature of their attacks—in so far as we can detect this from Patrick's rather confusing account—shows them as proud, conservative, uncompromising men. Patrick humbly introduces himself as 'the most illiterate and the least of all the faithful, and contemptible in the eyes of very many'. He has, he says, been derided as unfit for the task he has taken upon himself; his opponents claimed that his mission-work 'did not seem meet in their eyes, on account of my illiteracy'. Patrick was not illiterate in the normal sense of the word. But as his writings testify, he was not at ease in writing Latin: his sentences are clumsy, and he finds his words with difficulty, often resorting to biblical phrases as a means of expressing himself. He admits that in using Latin he is translating into a language not his own, whereas others have not only studied Law and the Scriptures, but have spoken the same language (i.e.

Latin) from infancy. It was the teaching of St Paul that a bishop should be a studious and knowledgeable man (1 Tim. 3.2), and evidently a high standard of education was an accepted prerequisite for at least the higher grades in the ecclesiastical hierarchy, even in the remote mountains of western Britain.

In other ways, too, Patrick's opponents were simply following St Paul's advice. Patrick mentions that some unspecified incident from his past was raised as an objection to his appointment as bishop, even by a friend who had once supported this appointment. It had been recommended by St Paul that a bishop must be of impeccable character (1 Tim. 5.21–2). Yet one suspects that the real reason underlying the attacks on Patrick was distaste for the unorthodox nature of his mission-work. In Gaul, the dedicated but unkempt St Martin of Tours had aroused similar opposition from the church establishment. Like St Martin, Patrick had taken the faith among peoples who had no respect for Roman culture and discipline. Ireland had not been occupied by the Romans, and the values of the Roman world there held no weight. It seems that, even in the highlands of western Britain, the clergy had come to value their dignity higher than the salvation of souls: better in their eyes that the Gospel should not be spread to barbarians like the Irish than that some ill-educated, uncouth enthusiast should degrade the office of bishop.

A group of fifth- to sixth-century inscriptions from Gwynedd show that there, too, the Christian officials were proud of their status, and were eagerly clinging on to whatever they had managed to acquire of Roman sophistication. An elaborate inscription at Llantrisant, Anglesey,[4] extols a bishop and his wife in extravagant terms: '. . . iva (or . . . ina), a most holy woman lies here, who was the very loving wife of Bivatig (irnus), servant of God, bishop (? or priest), and disciple of Paulinus, by race a . . . docian, and an example to all his fellow citizens and relatives both in character (and) in rule of life, (as also) of wisdom (which is better) than gold and gems.'[5] Another bishop, Sanctinus, is commemorated at Bodafon, Caernarvonshire,[6] while presbyters (priests) are remembered on two stones at Aberdaron.[7] Sometimes pride in the dignity of Roman office caused the bounds of propriety to be overstepped: at Llangian,

Caernarvonshire,[8] we find the early Christians commemorating someone as a '*medicus* (doctor)'—mention in an early Christian epitaph of the deceased man's secular profession is most irregular, though it had been a normal pagan practice. Somewhat similar is the statement on a stone at Penmachno that the commemorated man was the cousin of a magistrate, and was himself a 'citizen of Gwynedd'.[9] When St Patrick wrote his *Letter* to the British prince, Coroticus, denouncing his war-band for their slaughter of converted Irishmen, the worst insult he could hurl at them was to refuse to address them as 'my fellow-citizens or . . . the fellow-citizens of the holy Romans'. Patrick may have seemed a rebel to the conservative clergy, but his thinking, no less than theirs, was imbued with deep respect for Roman culture.

Gildas was a staunch supporter of Roman standards, but he had no time for the pride and complacency so often displayed by those who were eager for the prestige that went with high appointments in the church. Many of the British priests, he claims, live wicked lives, concerned purely with their own benefit. They curry favour with the rich, however impious, while scorning the righteous poor. They fail to give alms, and amuse themselves at public games, with scandalous stories, and even with women; they indulge themselves to excess. Clearly the clergy enjoyed a very privileged position: Gildas claims that some men, refused ordination at home, will seek it abroad, sometimes even selling all their possessions to obtain 'such display and incomparable dignity'. If this grandeur owed something to the splendour of the civic dignitaries of the Roman provinces upon whose organization the Church had modelled itself, it probably owed something too to the honoured place that religious specialists had always enjoyed in British society. The druids whom the Christian clergy replaced had been a highly educated, professional body, the right-hand men of princes, and accustomed to being supported in style. Interestingly, the headquarters of the druids had been in Gwynedd, the very area in which the stone monuments attest an early and grandiose branch of the church.

Even the clergy who were blameless in their own lives were, Gildas laments, stained with the sin of pride. Secure in their own righteousness, they lacked the zeal to urge their flocks to a

Christian way of life. Here, the basis of Gildas's complaint seems to be that the clergy fail to bring the headstrong native princes to book—as he so earnestly seeks to do by his castigation of them. Probably these clergy were simply more tolerant than Gildas of native custom, even where this was at variance with the teachings of the Roman Church. To Gildas, even bardic entertainment was execrable and unchristian.

Gildas was a reformer, an exceptional man who looked beyond the institutions in which the Church had clad itself to the ideals it was meant to serve. For him, it was not enough for the clergy to be learned and respected men: they must lead exemplary Christian lives, and by example and exhortation inspire their flocks to do the same. Most of the clergy would have seen nothing wrong with the way things were. The Church was secure, its ministers respected. The proud record of the Christian inscriptions speaks of believers well pleased with themselves.

Yet there were some devout men who were not satisfied to rest on their laurels within the comfortable Church establishment: Gildas is careful to exempt them from his denunciation, and says that he himself hopes to adopt their way of life before his death. Presumably Gildas is referring to monks. One of Gildas's grudges against Maelgwn, prince of Gwynedd, is that, after taking monk's vows, he had returned to his former way of life; and he speaks disgustedly of how Constantine of Damnonia had compounded a crime of murder by committing it in the guise of an abbot.

There is no evidence in Gildas or elsewhere that monks in the sixth-century British Church were anything other than a small minority. Patrick, in his *Confession*, mentioned that the sons and daughters of the Irish chiefs were becoming monks and virgins of Christ, but probably this meant no more than that they dedicated themselves individually to a chaste and virtuous life, not that they lived within religious communities. The earliest known monastery in Britain is that excavated at Tintagel, on the north coast of Cornwall, and dated by archaeologists to the late fifth century; in Gwynedd, the fifth- or early sixth-century inscription at Aberdaron recording the burial of the priest Senacus 'with a host of brethren' may suggest some sort of religious community.[10] Significantly, both these sites are coastal: for, as we have seen, monasticism, which had originated in the Eastern Mediterranean lands and had been further developed in Gaul, spread to Britain by the western sea-routes. This Eastern-derived monasticism differed considerably from the Benedictine and other developed forms of monasticism with which we are familiar. Monasticism was still at an experimental stage. Religious communities had developed in the Eastern deserts as more and more Christians fled to the deserts to follow the example of the influential early-fourth-century hermit, St Anthony, or to escape persecution. John Cassian wrote books of guidance for those intending to follow the religious life, and by the mid-fourth century monastic theory had spread to the West, where several communities were founded in Gaul. The basis of this early monasticism was a life of harsh self-denial, like that which the desert hermits had led. It was believed that, by subduing all worldly desires and all temptations of the spirit, the mind would be left free for the contemplation of God. Life was thus a constant struggle, a perpetual battle against the weaknesses of the flesh and the distractions of the devil. It was an individual struggle: the monks did not passively observe an imposed discipline, but each lived in his own cell and entered the fray on his own account.

The disadvantage of this individualism was that it could lead to excess. We need not doubt that the extreme ascetics saw devils, as their biographers claim. The weapons which the Christian militants used to conquer evil—sexual continence, fasting, prolonged sleepless vigils, recitation over and over again of the potent words of the Psalter—must have weakened mind and body to the very limits of health and sanity, and encouraged the very hallucinations they were intended to suppress. Only the very strongest could bear such trials without support. By settling in groups, the ascetics could give mutual support to each other; and soon rules were drawn up for individual communities, providing a framework of discipline which prevented extremism getting out of hand. The pursuit of the contemplative ideal by an individual living in isolation continued to be regarded as the highest form of the religious life; but it was thought suitable only for those who had first achieved perfection in the communal life.

The desert monks were primarily concerned with spiritual

warfare. Though organized physical labour, social responsibilities and intellectual pursuits did become acceptable elements in the religious life, their importance was limited. It was to escape such worldly concerns that the first monks had left their homes. But in western Europe, with the disintegration of the Roman Empire, social stability and scholarship deteriorated gravely, and the monasteries increasingly felt the need to supply the deficit. The monastery at Lérins in Gaul supplied several bishops, who after training in the monastery ventured out to serve and inspire society at large. In Italy in the sixth century, Cassiodorus not only made his monastery at Vivarium a centre of learning, but stressed the value of secular classics, which had been shunned by the early Church which would have nothing to do with pagan authors. Monastic life was infinitely diverse: normally the founder of a monastery would draw up a regime to be followed by those who entered his foundation. The sixth-century rule of St Benedict of Nursia, later to be so influential, was as yet but one rule among many.

Unfortunately, no single example of an early monastic rule from Britain has survived.[11] As at Tintagel, we may assume that the monks, like their predecessors in the East and in the early monasteries in Gaul, would have lived in individual cells. Bede mentions that the monks at Bangor-is-coed lived 'by the labour of their own hands'.[12] Gildas, in his attack on the clergy, makes no mention of monks taking any part in church administration: rather, his wish to share in their way of life before he dies suggests that they are completely withdrawn from the world—he will retire to a monastery once his reforming days are over.

As we shall see, asceticism continued to be valued in Wales up to and beyond Norman times; when, in the eleventh- and twelfth-century saints' *Lives*, we read accounts of the ascetic regimes followed by the saints, these tell us what a later age expected of its saints, rather than how they really lived. However, the *Life of St David* does seem to draw on an early monastic rule for its detailed description of life at St David's monastery.[13] Similarities between this rule and those drawn up by the eighth-to-ninth-century revivers of asceticism in the Irish Church suggest that in its present form the rule in fact dates from some centuries after

51

David's lifetime.[14] However, its authors may have been influenced by a genuine tradition of asceticism at St David's, dating back to the saint's own time: David acquired the nickname *Aquaticus* (water-drinker) in recognition of his bread-and-water regime.[15]

The regime described in St David's *Life* is uncompromisingly harsh. Like the monks Bede mentioned at Bangor-is-coed, the monks lived by the labour of their own hands: they scorned even to use animal-power, and yoked their own shoulders to the plough. Whatever time was left free from manual toil was filled by reading, writing, or prayer. The church bell was instantly obeyed, even if a scribe had to abandon his work with 'only the tip of a letter or even half the form of the same letter . . . written'. Long hours were spent in vigils, prayers, and prostrations. Poverty was absolute: no gifts were to be accepted, not even endowments from those entering as monks. Diet was severely restricted. In a society where life was already harsh enough by our standards, asceticism involved the most extreme hardship: monks obedient to such a rule would have been far removed from the calm, peaceful, robe-clad figures we tend to associate with the words 'monk' and 'nun'. Malnourished, weather-beaten, their labour-racked bodies clad only in 'clothes of mean quality, mainly skins', they would have looked more like shriftless derelicts. One doubts whether they would have found favour with the more conventional clergy, so proud of their civilized Roman ways. In the early days of the Irish church, a synod decreed that a clergyman seen without a tunic and without his hair cut in the Roman manner should be cast out from the church: one suspects that this emphasis on decent appearance would have been heartily approved of by the contemporary British clergy, who, as we have seen, were much concerned with their own dignity.

The fact that St David's became famed for the severity of its rule implies that its extreme asceticism was exceptional. A quite different reputation was acquired by St Illtud's monastery at Llantwit. In the ninth to eleventh centuries, Llantwit was an important cultural centre, as can be seen from the numerous stone crosses of high standard found on the site.[16] This may have led to a revival of interest in the site's founder, and in the twelfth

I CHRISTIAN STONE MONUMENTS

(a) An early memorial stone with Latin inscription commemorating Dervacus, son of Justus. (Detail on right.)

(b) A tenth- or eleventh-century stone bearing a symbolic representation of the crucifixion

II   A SCULPTED CROSS FROM MARGAM, GLAMORGAN

century a *Life of St Illtud* was written. But traditions about Illtud had been current well before the ninth century. In the *Life of St Samson*, probably dating from the early seventh century, the abbot Illtud is described as 'an illustrious master of the Britons', learned in Scripture and philosophy, and able to foretell the future (ch. 7); and Nennius's historical compilation includes a miracle connected with the saint. In *Lives* of various Breton saints, and in the *Life of St Illtud* itself, Illtud's reputation as a teacher is emphasized, and various other saints are listed as his disciples—including Gildas. Gildas, in his *De Excidio*, said that Maelgwn of Gwynedd was once taught by 'the refined teacher of almost the whole of Britain', and this may be a reference to Illtud. It seems that Illtud's monastery was from the beginning an important centre of learning, and perhaps, like Lérins in Gaul, served as a training-house for clergy. In so early a monastery the emphasis on scholarship would have been unusual. It may be that Illtud was educated in the secular schools which we assume still survived in those areas of lowland Britain as yet not overrun by the Saxons, and was reluctant to abandon his learning with the rest of worldly preoccupations when he took to the religious life. The *Life of St Samson* says that Illtud was ordained presbyter by St Germanus of Auxerre: if this happened during Germanus's visits to Britain to combat Pelagianism, it would connect Illtud with the cultured world of the native rhetoricians who met Germanus in debate.[17]

What happened to the organization of the church after the immediate post-Roman period is anything but clear: until the eve of the Welsh Church's submission to Canterbury we have only a few hints to suggest the course of church development. In Ireland, the late sixth and seventh centuries saw a wide-scale expansion of monasticism. Monasticism provided scope for the individualism so beloved of the Irish; and it proved readily adaptable to their social structure, in which the kin-group was the important unit. A monastery was vested in the founder's kin, who had the right to appoint successive abbots. When monks ventured forth from the major monasteries to set up satellite foundations, these remained under the control of the mother house: thus scattered groupings of monasteries were established, and the abbots became powerful administrators. More and more of the clergy were also living a communal religious life, and many bishops, too, retaining their sacramental functions but stripped of administrative duties, lived as monks, obedient to the abbots.

Did the same monastic expansion, and the same administrative changes take place across the sea in western Britain? Even allowing for exaggeration, Bede's statement that there were over 2,400 monks at Bangor-is-coed (near Chester) early in the seventh century,[18] and the tradition that thousands of 'saints' were buried on Bardsey Island imply an enthusiastic response to the monastic challenge. When the Normans arrived in Wales in the late eleventh century, they found groups of *claswyr* (men of the Church) established at the major churches, headed by abbots whose title surely points to their monastic origins. The *clasau*, or mother churches, were responsible for subordinate or daughter churches, a pattern which is similar to the monastic groupings found in Ireland. If in Wales, as in Ireland, succession to the monasteries had remained in the hands of the founder's kin, this would explain why the names of the founders (the saints) were remembered.

However, the expansion in Irish monasticism was exceptional: it was not confined to Ireland, but overflowed into western Europe, where Irish monks helped restore the Latin culture destroyed by the barbarian invasions. The British monks were never so influential. Though there were some large and successful monasteries, these may have been few and far between. Some abbots were minor potentates, but abbots do not seem to have replaced the bishops as administrators. In the probably early-seventh-century *Life of St Samson*, the bishop Dubricius appears to be in control of the monasteries within his diocese: for instance, when the abbot Piro falls into a pit after having too much to drink, and dies, it is the bishop who tells the monks how to act, and who summons a council to elect Piro's successor (ch. 36). Recent analysis of the eighth-century charters in the *Book of Lichfield* and of the charters in the twelfth-century *Book of Llandaff* (which seem to be based on earlier records) suggests that diocesan sees persisted in South Wales;[19] moreover, it seems that when the Welsh bishops did take to the monastic life they not only retained their diocesan sees, but in addition became the administrators of the monasteries and their subject foundations. Thus in the eighth century, witnesses to grants recorded in the margins of the *Book of Lichfield* included a bishop of St Teilo, who was both bishop and abbot; while Asser, talking of the monastery and *paruchia* of St David's, makes no reference to an abbot, only to the bishop. In the Welsh Laws the chief ecclesiastical court is that of the bishop.

For most of the life of the Celtic Church, bishops were apparently far more numerous in Wales than the four to which their numbers had been reduced by the time the Anglo-Normans took over control of the Church in Wales. Gildas's general references to bishops imply that they were a sizeable class, while later we find, for intance, that the Welsh Laws make mention of seven *esgoptai* (bishops' houses) in Dyfed, whereas the Welsh annals, recording the death of Bishop Elfoddw in A.D. 809, call him 'chief bishop in the land of Gwynedd'. There is no evidence that the bishops were organized into a formal hierarchy, though some bishops, like Elfoddw and like Nobis, Bishop of St David's, whom Asser calls 'archbishop', would be more influential than others—it was Elfoddw, incidentally, who was credited with persuading the Church in Wales to conform to the Roman Easter date. The idea that there should be a primate of the Welsh Church, an archbishop to whom all other bishops owed obedience, developed only under Norman influence. But there had been some movement towards centralization. There are signs that by the eve of the Norman Conquest the power within the Welsh Church had become concentrated in a few major foundations: the late stone crosses, for intance, are clustered round a few major centres. Similarly, control of the Church seems to have become concentrated in the hands of a few major bishops, who were striving to acquire extensive territorial dioceses, such as existed elsewhere in the Western Church. The earlier saints' *Lives* reflect the resultant rivalries between the Welsh foundations: for example, the *Life* of the Irish saint Finnian and the *Life of St David* both tell a story of how David was declared chief among three eminent Welsh saints. Here in embryo were the claims to primacy which, under the Norman bishop, Bernard, St David's was to elaborate into a serious case for her metropolitan status, a case which she took to Rome.[20]

The Normans arrived in Wales at the very time when the popes were turning their traditional prestige as guardians of the relics of the saints—especially of St Peter, holder of the keys of Heaven—into practical authority over the Church as a whole. Uniformity in practice and belief had long been an ideal, but political disruption had hindered communications, and even the holding of General Church Councils had been impracticable for long periods at a time. Celtic church organization had diverged from that established in the rest of the Church because of the early date at which it had been introduced and the Celtic Church's subsequent isolation—the same factors that had left the Celts following outdated practices in calculating Easter. Similarly, the Celtic monasteries, because they had been founded at an early stage in the development of monasticism in the West, and because they were specially adapted to Celtic society, displayed certain features which appeared highly irregular to those familiar with the Benedictine monasticism that eventually became prevalent elsewhere. Though in the eighth century the Celtic Church in Wales conformed to Roman practice in calculating the date of Easter, and probably in some other details such as the form of tonsure,[21] this did not mean that it abandoned all its old ways. It was influenced, not controlled, by Rome.

The Normans were horrified to find in the Welsh Church married clergy, laymen holding office as abbots, and the handing down of abbacies and other ecclesiastical appointments from father to son: but all these 'abuses' can be explained as inheritances from early church custom, or as the result of the *clasau*'s monastic origins.

Married clergy had been perfectly acceptable in the primitive Church, and some monks too continued to live with their wives and children after taking to the religious life. St Augustine, in the early fifth century, denounced in his *De Haeresibus* the arrogance of a group, the 'Apostolics', who 'rejected all from their communion, who had either wives or estates, of which sort the Catholic Church had many, both monks and clergy'. There was nothing exceptional in St Patrick being the son and grandson of men in orders. But ascetic attitudes slowly gathered weight. In the fifth century the papacy came out in support of celibacy for the higher clerical grades, and by the late sixth century it was usual in Gaul for bishops to separate from their wives at the time of consecration. At this time the British Church was in touch with the church in Gaul, and Gildas says some British bishops obtained their consecration there; but the British bishops seem to have continued to live with their wives. Gildas criticizes the unchastity of some bishops and their children; citing St Paul's intruction that a bishop is to have 'his children subjected with all chastity', he says that 'the chastity of the parents' is imperfect, 'if the children be not also endued with the same'.[22] Clearly Gildas is visualizing a situation where bishops would still be living with their families. It seems that what he is criticizing is simply their failure to conform to St Paul's requirement that they should be faithful to a single wife, and their failure to enforce the same standard upon their children. Two early Christian monuments in Anglesey record the burial of the wives of bishops: at Llantrisant, 'the very loving wife of Bivatig(irnus) ... bishop' is commemorated,[23] while at Llansadwrn 'blessed ... Saturninus' is said to be interred with his 'saintly wife'.[24] The emphasis in these sixth-century inscriptions on the relationship between husband and wife is surely incompatible with their having separated when the husband entered the service of the Church.

In later centuries, we hear from time to time of the children of clergymen. For example, Cuhelin, son of Nobis, bishop of St Teilo, witnesses a grant recorded in the eighth century in the *Book of Lichfield*. Sometimes this need mean no more than that the father had been married before he took orders. More telling is the evidence that sometimes the connection between a church and a particular family might persist through several generations. In the eleventh and twelfth centuries, the sons and grandsons of Sulien, bishop of St David's, a family based at Llanbadarn Fawr (near Aberystwyth), held ecclesiastical posts in Llanbadarn, St David's, and the surrounding area. As children, these men would have been brought up within the Church (for instance, we know that Sulien's grandson, the son of Rhigyfarch who wrote the *Life of St David*, was entrusted to the clergy of Llanbadarn for upbringing): it is somewhat far-fetched to imagine that they would then sandwich in a swift, son-producing marriage before accepting clerical appointments. When the Normans entered Wales, they found non-celibate clergy at many of the *clasau*. This is not surprising: the movement towards celibacy in the Western Church was a gradual process, which experienced many setbacks. One would expect that the movement would at times have had some impact in Wales, as it did in Ireland; but possibly the disruption of the Viking raids had encouraged a general slackening of standards, a return to the old tolerance of married clergymen.

The honouring of women in several early Christian inscriptions shows that they were respected members of the Christian community. Presumably in western Britain, as in Ireland and Gaul, women as well as men responded to the spread of monastic ideas by taking to the religious life, some with their families, some on their own account. In the *Life of Samson* (ch. 29), when Samson's father has decided that he and his wife should devote themselves to God's service, it is his wife who urges: 'Let not only me and thee . . . serve God, but let us link together all our children in the service of God and let all that is ours become wholly God's.' Women are included among the Welsh saints, most famous being St Gwenfrewi (Winifred), the patron of the healing well from which Holywell in Flintshire takes its name. Women in early Welsh literature—Branwen and Rhiannon, for intance, in the Four Branches of the *Mabinogi*[25]—have minds and wills of their own: the society which made heroines of such women is unlikely to have denied women at least some measure of participation in the Church. However, by the time the *Lives* of the Welsh saints were written, the strong anti-feminism of the Normans was making itself felt. St Illtud's biographer uses Illtud's wife, Trinihid, to illustrate the poisonousness of women. When St Illtud is commanded by an angel to abandon his military career and turn to the religious life, he is asleep beside Trinihid. The angel tells him to look at her naked body and recognize its lack of worth. Waking from his dream, Illtud sends his wife to see to their horses; obediently, she gets up, and he sees her standing naked before him. The woman he had once loved now appears to Illtud as 'a fatal source of ruin': without any explanation, he drives her from their bed. The rejected Trinihid settles down to lead a chaste and pious life; but the hagiographer has not yet finished with her. Women are so dangerous, it seems, that even chaste nuns, such as Trinihid had become, must be allowed nowhere near men serving God: when Trinihid ventures to visit her former husband, 'owing to her improper visit she lost her sight.' At Illtud's intercession, her sight is restored, but 'Nevertheless her countenance was not afterwards so fair as before, affected with spots and pallor, and pallid as though ill with fever.' (*Life of St Illtud*, paras. 4–5 and 16.)

We know from the *Life of St Samson* that the hereditary succession to ecclesiastical appointments which the Normans were so shocked to find in the *clasau* dated back to the time of the early monasteries. A story in the *Life* tells of the jealousy of two of St Illtud's nephews of Illtud's affection for Samson; one of them, a presbyter, is especially jealous, because he fears that he will lose 'his hereditary right in the monastery' (ch. 16). Their resentment is so great that they try to poison Samson. We have mentioned that, in Irish monasteries, the kin of the founder controlled the succession to the abbacy; if they could not supply a suitable candidate, then the right passed to the kin of the donor of the site. This system was a natural result of the overriding importance of the kin-group in Celtic society. It was a person's descent that played the main part in determining his status in society and his role in life. Just as princes would be drawn from a royal family, so druids and blacksmiths and other specialists would be drawn from families traditionally connected with these callings; and the same connection with family came to influence appointments within the church.

At first sight, this sytem would seem to be at variance with Christianity's emphasis on the value of the individual soul: ideally, ability and piety should be the only qualifications for ecclesiastical appointments. But ability was not easily come by. Church officials were required to move freely among the upper classes of society, and they needed to have acquired a reasonable standard of education, including knowledge of Latin. The advantage of the hereditary succession to appointments was that care could be taken to ensure that the heirs were suitably prepared for their future role. The *Life of St Cadog* relates how the saint, having no children of his own, accepts a three-year-old child as a foster-son, who grows up to become Cadog's 'successor' (paras. 14 and 49). Since ability is itself in part hereditary, and since there would normally be more than one possible heir (so that the less suitable could be overlooked), there is no reason to suppose that the quality of abbots and clergy suffered greatly from the system. Like the Bachs and the Huxleys, some exceptional families like that of Bishop Sulien could maintain high standards of dedication and scholarship over several generations. Much of the land in Wales was held in joint possession by the kin-group; but even land that was appropriated by individuals or families was subject to set laws of inheritance, and even if it was abandoned the heirs of the original owner retained the right to it for nine generations. The predominant part played by the kin in land-ownership explains why the kin of the donors of Christian sites, as well as the founders' kin, expected to retain some interest in the foundations. Princes who gave land for Christian burial-grounds or settlements were procuring the benefits of Christian ministry and burial for their families: they would treat the sites virtually as royal possessions, an attitude the Church came to resent, as we see from the strong emphasis in the saints' *Lives* on the Church's right to be exempt from royal demands. When a whole family handed over their lands to the Church and took to the religious life, as we find St Samson's family doing in the *Life of St Samson*, the founder's and donor's kin would be identical; if most of the kin continued to live in families and work their land, supporting the small group who lived a strict communal religious life, this would explain some distinctive features in Irish and Welsh church organization.[26] By the seventh and eighth centuries, we find families of laymen working the lands of Irish monasteries under the overlordship of the abbot: their eldest sons were educated in the monastic schools, providing future members for the little community of men in orders which formed the nucleus of the monastery. The Welsh *clasau* look very like developments from this sort of establishment. By the eleventh and twelfth centuries, few of the *claswyr* were in orders, but this may simply reflect the difficulties of maintaining a reasonable standard of education.[27]

Some of the lay abbots to whom the Normans objected may have gained their posts simply because the kin connected with the *clas* could supply no more suitable candidate. The Welsh clung tenaciously to their rights to hereditary succession, as the Norman reformers of the Church were to find. As late as *c*.1230 the Annals of Tewkesbury Abbey record that there had been disputes about the church at Llanddewi Brefi 'between Peter, Abbot of Tewkesbury, and certain persons who wished that a brother of William, lately parson there, and his kin should succeed him by hereditary right, as is the custom among the Welsh'. However, the system was open to abuse. Men wishing to secure exemption for their families from secular dues may have nominally handed over their lands to the Church, while keeping almost all the income from the lands for themselves; other lay abbots may have seized church possessions, leaving the *claswyr* to subsist on the church dues alone.

When church appointments were dependent on a person's family, it was inevitable that a person's status in secular society largely determined his status within the Church. But in theory a priest or monk merited high status regardless of his background: thus the Welsh Laws provided that 'a clerk who is a bondman, the day he receives the tonsure' becomes 'a freeman that night'.[28] In practice the chances of this happening were remote, for scholarship was one of the three arts which the laws forbade a bondsman to teach his son, for the very reason that 'if his lord be passive until the tonsure be given to the scholar . . . no one can enslave [him] after that.'[29]

Some ascetics sought to prevent their worldly status accompanying them into the religious life. The monastic rule section in the *Life of St David* forbids the usual acceptance of endowments from entrants to the monastery, for it recognizes that those able to give more might feel superior to those giving less, or might consider manual work beneath their dignity (ch. 30). A more usual solution was for a person to avoid the social structure of either a secular or a religious community, by devoting himself to God in solitude as an anchorite.

Giraldus Cambrensis claimed in his *Description of Wales* that

61

'Nowhere are hermits and anchorites to be found who practise greater abstinence and lead a more spiritual life' (I. 18). According to the classification of the seventh-century writer Isidore of Seville, hermits were those who sought out remote deserts to live; anchorites were those who withdrew to an individual cell after first achieving perfection in the communal religious life. It was the retreat of hermits to the deserts of Egypt and the Near East that had sparked off the development of monasticism, and the monastic ideas that spread to Britain involved the individual as well as the communal religious life. It became conventional for the authors of the saints' *Lives* to claim that their heroes had spent periods as hermits or anchorites, but at least we can accept that the reference in the early *Life of St Samson* to the saint's retreat to a cave in the Severn valley is likely to be authentic. In the late sixth century, the Abbot of Bangor-is-coed consulted a recluse on how the meeting with St Augustine should be handled. Apparently retreats might either be permanent, or for temporary spiritual rejuvenation: many monasteries had caves or islands or other suitable places near by, where members of the community could isolate themselves from time to time, as St Cadog is said to have retreated from Llancarfan to the islands of Barry and Flat Holm during Lent. Anchoritism must have creamed off many of the truly devout from the churches and monasteries, leaving men of a more practical bent to run church affairs. Even the Normans were impressed by the dedication of the anchorites, and they continued to be an important element in the medieval Welsh Church.

The Christian recluses appealed directly to the native imagination. These unkempt dwellers in the caves and woods were the ecclesiastical equivalent of the 'wild men of the woods' of Celtic legend, who were credited with prophetic powers. In British tradition, the type was represented by Merfyn Frych—the character later transformed into the Merlin of Arthurian romance.[30] The story told how Merfyn, driven mad by battle-shock, fled to the woods, where he lived like a savage, uttering prophecies. The ascetic enthusiasm of the Christian solitaries might bring them to the very verge of madness; and the value placed on their advice (as when the recluse was consulted about the negotiations with

Augustine) suggests that they had inherited the role of the pagan prophets.

The example of the renowned hermits, St Paul and St Anthony, proved influential in Wales as elsewhere in encouraging respect for the solitary religious life. The lowest panel on the ninth-century cross-slab at Nash, Glamorgan,[31] depicts the meeting of St Paul and St Anthony in the desert, a popular scene found also on stone monuments in Northumbria, Scotland, and Ireland. According to St Jerome's *Life of Paul*, the two hermits (Anthony aged 113, Paul aged 90) had been so determined to prove their humility when they met, that they had spent all day quarrelling about which of them should have the honour of breaking a loaf of bread miraculously brought to them by a raven. Eventually they both took hold of the loaf, and pulled. The carving at Nash shows the two hermits, with staffs in their hands, sitting facing each other at their meeting.

4

The Church within Society

The British princes were not administrators, but figureheads. Society ran itself along customary lines, with the kin-groups enforcing good conduct on their members, masters on their bondsmen and slaves. A prince was a symbol of his people's unity and identity. By his wealth—by the size of his household, the generosity of his gifts and patronage—he displayed his people's prosperity; by leading his war-band into battle he not only protected his people, but inspired them with confidence in their own might, and impressed outsiders with their prowess. When challenge from enemies was lacking, raids for cattle or women served to quench the vital thirst for glory. Such are the princes, the *tyranni*, berated by Gildas: fierce, proud men pursuing their own pleasures, feasting and womanizing and brawling, fighting each other instead of uniting against the Saxon threat, preferring to hear their own praises rather than the word of God.

It was essential for the Church to seek the favour of the princes, right from the early days of the conversion. A missionary needed the local prince's approval if he was not to be driven away from his lands. Once the prince was converted, his household would follow suit—including the members of his war-band, aristocratic young men who would be the heads of their families in the next generation. With these men converted, the spreading of the faith to the lesser ranks of society was just a matter of time—though one suspects that for a long time their Christianity would be purely nominal. The Church's Latin culture can have seemed no less than magical to the uneducated, with its mysterious symbols carved on stone, and the incomprehensible words of hymns and chants. The people were used to being excluded from a culture of which they could only wonder at the outward signs: the complexities of pagan mythology and religion had also been the province of a court-based learned élite.

Provided ordinary folk were given rudimentary Christian instruction, and were baptized into the Church, the church officials may well have considered their duties towards them at an end. It was with the aristocracy and above all with the princes that the bishops and other church dignitaries, learned and cultured men, could develop a relationship fruitful for both sides.

The Church brought to the princes' courts some of the benefits of Roman culture, which the princes were so keen to acquire: literacy, Latin-based learning, the splendours of church ceremonial with its splendid vestments and use of precious wines and oils. And the price of these refinements was no longer submission to political conquest, but merely adherence to a faith which was itself attractive, promising forgiveness, however great one's sins, and perpetual heavenly glory to follow what was already for the princes a glorious life on earth.

Only slowly could Christian morality, nurtured in the very different Roman world, be expected to alter the customary Celtic way of life. Gildas, in his denunciation of the sixth-century British princes, saw in Christian terms, as vices and virtues, attributes which were all alike the product of the princes' Celtic heritage. They indulged in pointless squabbles because fighting was their expected occupation; they were generous because a Celtic prince was judged by his generosity. So few written records of early British history survived that Gildas's diatribe was fed on eagerly by later students of the past; and Maelgwn of Gwynedd, the prince he condemned most strongly, became enshrined in tradition as the archetypal persecutor of the Church. In the *Lives* of the Welsh saints, the persecution of a saint by a tyrant is a common story-type: ultimately the wrong-doer is brought to repentance, and pays for his obduracy with generous grants of land or privileges to the saint's foundations. Maelgwn appears especially often in this role—in the *Life of St Cadog*, for instance (para. 23), and in the *Life of St Cybi* (paras. 17–19). We should not take these fables seriously: in the twelfth century, when most of these *Lives* were written, the Church needed to defend its lands and rights, and these stories were designed to authenticate the Church's possessions by claiming that they had been granted by eminent figures. Any name seems to have sufficed, provided it was well known. The British hero, Macsen Wledig, was cast in the tyrant/persecutor role in a medieval Cornish mystery play;[1] while Arthur is the tyrant in the *Life of St Padarn* (para. 21), though he appears in his usual hero role in the *Lives of St Illtud* (para. 2) and *St Carannog* (paras. 4–5).

In reality, princes and Church in Gildas's time seem to have been on good terms—too good, in Gildas's view, since he feels the clergy should be bringing the princes to book. Earlier, St Patrick in his *Letter to Coroticus* had criticized the 'holy men' at the court of the British prince Coroticus for the same failure to enforce Christian standards: they should, he said, avoid eating or drinking with Coroticus and his soldiers, and refuse to pay court to them, or to receive their alms, until the prince and his soldiers had done penance for their crimes against Patrick's Irish converts. The disadvantage in this sort of spiritual sending-to-Coventry was that an impious or unscrupulous ruler could simply ignore such threats, either abandoning Christianity altogether, or (like Henry VIII) obtaining the services of clergy who could be trusted to support his own point of view.[2] Throughout western Europe at this time 'The bishops were appointed by the kings and obedient to them, even if the kings themselves were heretics.'[3] The bishops who are accused by Gildas of buying their appointments from the native princes rather than from the Apostles were in no way exceptional.

The princes retained their powerful hold over the Welsh bishops (and, indeed, over the Church as a whole) throughout the life of the Celtic Church. In the late ninth century, Asser tells us that his colleagues at St David's agreed to his spending half each year at the English King Alfred's court because they hoped that, by securing Alfred's friendship, they would suffer 'fewer tribulations and injuries from King Hemeid',[4] who often ravaged St David's, sometimes expelling the bishop himself.

The Norman kings and archbishops did not deprive the Welsh princes of their power over the bishops without a struggle, especially in the North. Hervé, the first Norman appointment to the bishopric of Bangor, was driven out in 1093, and Gruffydd ap Cynan of Gwynedd succeeded in preventing not only him but also the next Norman appointee becoming bishop. Eventually a

Welsh candidate, David, was made bishop of Bangor. But the victory was a hollow one: when David was consecrated in 1120, he professed obedience to Canterbury.

In Ireland, there are signs that the power of the kings over the Church greatly increased from the ninth century onwards, quite possibly as a result of the Viking raids. The Church was in need of protection; and the chaotic political situation would have left the kings free to interfere with impunity in church affairs, whether by enforcing their own choice in church appointments, or by helping themselves to some of the wealth of the churches and monasteries—wealth which would otherwise, after all, fall into Viking hands. In Wales, King Hemeid's harassment of St David's may have been symptomatic of a similar increase in the Church's vulnerability. With the advance of the Normans into Wales, that vulnerability was renewed. The eleventh- and twelfth-century *Lives* of the Welsh saints refer to recent attacks on the Church from all sides: by English and Danish troops (in pre-Norman times); by the Normans; by the Welsh themselves; by any of these enemies acting in alliance. For instance, a long series of posthumous miracles credited to St Gwynllyw is actually based on incidents involving attacks on the Church near to the hagiographer's own time: these incidents include a piratical raid by Norsemen from the Orkneys, accompanied by the exiled King Gruffydd of Gwynedd; a punitive invasion of Glamorgan by the English under Earl Harold (later, King Harold of Hastings fame); and another punitive raid by the Normans, led by William Rufus on the orders of his father, William the Conqueror (*Life of St Gwynllyw*, paras. 12, 13, and 15). In a battle described in the *Life of St Illtud*, Welsh rebels against the Normans are the enemy, and Illtud's clergy and the neighbouring people unite to defeat them (para. 26). The Church is caught up in secular politics, and when an area is attacked, its churches and monasteries are not always granted the immunity they claim, even if the raiders are Christians.

The accounts in the saints' *Lives* of attacks upon the saints' churches have a cautionary flavour: would-be molesters of the Church must reckon with the anger of the saint. Significantly, most of the *Lives* were produced in south and east Wales, the areas where the Norman advance made most progress. Often, the *Lives* defensively stress the protection which the saints' foundations are entitled to enjoy from kings and princes. Caradog Braichbras, who had allegedly sat 'in the chief seat of the kingdom of the Britons', was said to have declared that St Padarn's churches, both in Wales and in Brittany, were to be immune from interference: they were to be 'as islands in a great sea'. Dreadful penalties were to result if 'any king, or king's son, or leader shall have made this law void' (*Life of St Padarn*, para. 22). In the early twelfth century, St Padarn's chief foundation, Llanbadarn Fawr, had fallen into Norman hands: the *clas* was disbanded, and its endowments given to the Benedictines of St Peter's, Gloucester, who sent monks to set up a monastic cell. But after the death of Henry I in 1135, the Welsh succeeded in driving the Normans from Ceredigion, and the *claswyr* returned to Llanbadarn; it was another hundred years before the *clas* there disappeared from record. The hagiographer's claim of the inviolability of St Padarn's churches was perhaps calculated to make the monks of Gloucester uneasy in their possession of Llanbadarn: at any rate, it is expressive of the spirit with which the *claswyr* fought back against their eviction.

The relationship between princes and the clergy would be at its closest for those clergy who ministered to the princes' households. Several early churches are close to princes' courts. In Anglesey, the church of Llangadwaladr, now peacefully remote in its country churchyard, stands on the site where the kings of Gwynedd once worshipped: their court was but two miles away, at Aberffraw.[5] Set in the nave wall facing the entrance to the church is a stone commemorating in what is still remarkably clear lettering: 'King Catamanus, wisest and most renowned of all kings'.[6] This is the King Cadfan who ruled Gwynedd in the early seventh century, whose son Cadwallon formed an alliance with Penda of Mercia against the growing menace of Northumbrian power, winning great success before he was killed in battle near Hexham in A.D. 633. It is Cadfan's grandson, Cadwaladr, who is honoured as the founder of the church at Llangadwaladr, and perhaps it was he who had the memorial inscribed. Nash-Williams sees in the 'grandiloquent phraseology' of the inscription a plain echo of 'the formal language of the imperial Byzantine court':[7] however much the sophistication of Byzantium and Rome might be beyond the wildest imaginings of the native princes, the Church's cultural contacts at least enabled them to hear of and yearn towards a glory greater than their own.

In Glamorgan, we find in the late ninth and tenth centuries another, less pretentious dynasty enjoying a special connection with the local church. At Llantwit Major, three sculptured crosses bear inscriptions commemorating kings. The first is a fine monument, perhaps the work of an Irish craftsman, which proclaims in carefully executed lettering: '. . . This cross Houelt prepared for the soul of Res his father.'[8] Presumably this is the Hywel ap Rhys who we know ruled Glywysing (the kingdom which contained Llantwit) in the late ninth century. The kings commemorated on the other two crosses (or rather, cross-shafts, for the heads of the crosses have been lost), Samson and Juthahel, may have belonged to the same dynasty, though no other reference to them has survived. Interestingly, these kings are not each assigned a monument to themselves. King Samson is commemorated along with Illtud, Samuel, and Ebisar; and the sponsor of the monument, another Samson, is careful to point out in the inscription that the cross is for his own soul, too.[9] Rather than dominating the cross, the inscription is fitted into small panels between the panels of key-pattern and plaitwork and other designs with which the cross-shaft is embellished. The inscription commemorating King Juthahel suggests the order of priorities: 'In the name of God the most high begins the cross of the Saviour, which Abbot Samson prepared for his own soul and for the soul of King Juthahel and (for the souls) of Artmail and Tecain.'[10] Stone-carving had become a specialized ecclesiastical craft, with centres like Llantwit apparently supporting schools of craftsmen. No doubt the local kings were important benefactors of the church, helping to make such display possible; and no doubt they expected to receive ministry from and to be buried and commemorated at Llantwit. But the commemoration of laymen has become a secondary purpose of the stone monuments: they are now grandiose expressions of the Church's dignity, dedicated to the glory of God and of his ministers on earth.

It is quite conceivable that blood-relationship explains the inclusion of several people (kings, clergy, and laymen) in the same inscription. Even when the local dynasty did not have a special interest in a church through the founder or donor having been one of their kin, what more likely recruiting-ground for the officials of a prestigious church than the family of the local prince? The abbot of such a foundation would have enjoyed a life comparable with that of the prince himself: he too would have toured his lands to collect tribute, he too would have defended and sought to extend his possessions and power, he too would have patronized artists, and entertained a multitude of guests at his table. The saints were usually said to have come from noble families, and sometimes, like Gwynllyw, Lord of Gwynlliog, and his son Cadog, 'abbot and prince over Gwynlliog' (*Life of St Cadog*, para. 18), to have been rulers themselves.

Baptism, whereby catechumens died to sin and were born anew into the faith, was perhaps the most important service the Church provided for laymen.[11] It would be preceded by elementary religious instruction. Since the Church had a virtual monopoly of literacy, and manuscripts were in any case valuable and scarce commodities, teaching would be oral: at best, the people may have learnt the Creed, the Lord's Prayer, a psalm or two, and have heard a few stories from the Old and New Testaments.

After baptism, the layman would be expected to conform to Christian standards of conduct. The system that had developed in the primitive Church to cope with breaches of Christian morality was that of confession and penance. At first, these rites were performed in public, in obedience to the apostolic direction, 'Confess your faults one to another' (James 5.16). Later, private penance became accepted, whereby sins were confided to a personal spiritual director, who would then advise an appropriate penance. It was private penance that took root in the Celtic churches; and in Ireland, penitentials (lists of offences and appropriate penances) were compiled. These borrowed from John Cassian (the writer whose works proved influential in spreading monastic theory to Western Europe) the concept of sin as the disease of the soul:

sins, like physical ailments, could be classified, and assigned causes and cures. The western British Christians apparently contributed to the development of penitential literature, for the Irish Columbanus, author of an influential penitential, says that Venianus, author of an earlier penitential on which his own is based, consulted Gildas on the penance proper for monks who left their monasteries without permission. Columbanus left Ireland to travel widely on the Continent, and his penitential laid the basis of the system of penance followed in the medieval Church.

Even in the earliest of surviving British poems, the North British *Gododdin*[12] (quite possibly seventh-century or even earlier in origin, though added to in later years), we find mention of Christian penance. The poem concerns a raid against the Anglo-Saxon settlers by the war-band of a British prince: the warriors will make blood flow, even though they have to do penance for it. The penitential system was above all realistic: it recognized the inevitability, especially in secular life, of moral imperfections, and it provided a means of atoning for such breaches of the Christian code. The war-band of the *Gododdin* were Christians fighting heathens: yet technically the Christian code decreed that all killing was wrong. Penance resolved the dilemma.

This is not to say that penance was taken lightly. The Celtic penitentials are excessively harsh:[13] they impose all manner of physical deprivations—fasting, immersion in cold water, sleeping on a bed of nettles. The most serious offences were punished by exile, the ultimate in suffering in a society where a person's kin and status were his chief source of maintenance, protection, and self-respect. Not surprisingly, before long the custom of commutation of penance developed, whereby the full penance was replaced by a shorter alternative: if the full penances had ever been imposed on any extensive scale one suspects they would have disrupted normal life to an impossible degree!

As personal spiritual advisers, the confessors could become influential counsellors of the princes—the role the druids had once fulfilled. A story in the *Life of St Cadog* tells how Maelgwn of Gwynedd, brought by a miracle to repent of his hostility towards Cadog's lands, promises the saint: 'to-day I choose thee to be my

71

confessor, if it shall be wellpleasing to thee, above all others among the men of the South' (para. 23). When later Maelgwn's son, Rhun, led an expedition to the South, his father instructed him and his troops 'that they should not inflict any injury on saint Cadog, because he was his confessor, and that they should not take from any of his land even one beast of smallest value without his permission' (para. 24).

Christianity had a modifying effect on customary Celtic law. By the time the Welsh Laws were codified (reputedly in the reign of Hywel Dda (ruled A.D. 918–52), though we possess no text earlier than the mid-twelfth century) the idea that crime was not just an offence against the kin-group concerned, but against the community as a whole was taking root. Payment of compensation was replacing the blood-feud as the penalty for murder, and a hierarchy of courts had been set up. Much of this modernization must be credited to influence from the developing Anglo-Saxon theory of justice, but this was itself influenced by Christian morality. It was the Church's literacy that made compilation and writing down of laws possible; it was the Church which did its best to stop the blood-feud (for what was the use of imposing penance for murder, if the slain man's kin were liable to slaughter the penitent out of hand?). The synods at which church legislation was agreed had shown how codes of behaviour could be based on rules reached by agreement and confirmed in writing, not just on customary usage.

The Church had its own courts to administer justice: according to the Welsh Laws these range from that of the abbot for his tenants to the bishop's court. The establishment of a comprehensive hierarchy of ecclesiastical courts in Wales, with Rome as the ultimate court of appeal, was the work of the Norman reformers: no doubt the earlier organization had been more haphazard. We catch a glimpse of an early court in the *Life of St Cadog*. Whereas the later saints' *Lives* from south-east Wales recognize the authority of the episcopal court of Llandaff, the late-eleventh-century *Life of St Cadog* pre-dates the ascendancy of Llandaff. It is concerned with the right of Llancarfan to exercise its own judicial authority. St Cadog, about to be miraculously spirited away to a monastery in Sicily, first gives his people instructions about how affairs are to be managed at Llancarfan:

> I order you this in the name of the Lord, that no mundane
> powerful king or bishop or nobleman ever judge over you as to
> any controversy or injury. But if any one shall inflict any crime
> (or, loss) against you, or any of you injure another . . . let your
> judges be from among yourselves . . . and let them decide truth
> according to the true finding of a synod and the procedure of
> my judicial book, which I have written (para. 37).

The court is to meet under a hazel tree which Cadog is said to
have planted. The hagiographer's assertion of Llancarfan's
freedom from secular or episcopal judicial authority smacks of a
reaction to Norman encroachment on Llancarfan's rights—but
such a reaction would have been pointless if Llancarfan had had
no rights to lose.

One of the charters appended to the *Life of St Cadog* illustrates
the sort of justice Llancarfan would have meted out. It tells how
Euan Buurr had slain two of his nephews, and was cursed by
Cadog and Illtud so that he was forced to come to them and
confess his crime. The saints ordered him to 'redeem the crime of
homicide', and accordingly compensation in the form of gifts of
land was paid to the Church by kings who were presumably
Euan's kin, and thus sharers in his guilt. But material compensation, such as a lay court would demand, was not enough. Spiritual
atonement was also required: Euan was commanded to do penance for fourteen years (para. 57). We need not suppose that this
detailed account is an authentic record from the time of the saints
(though it may be based on some brief early record); but as title
for the Church's possessions, the charter was intended to appear
authentic, and presumably shows how things were done when the
Life itself was written.

Very different is the bizarre story of Sawyl Penuchen (*Life of
St Cadog*, para. 16). Sawyl, like his Biblical namesake Saul, is said
to have persecuted the Church: St Cadog responds to his seizure
of food and drink from Llancarfan by preaching patience to the
clergy, but at the same time imposes a brutal punishment on the
tyrant. When Sawyl and his followers have fallen into a drunken
sleep, half of their beards and hair are to be shaved, and the lips

and ears of their horses are to be cut. (As it turns out, this punishment is somewhat redundant, since immediately afterwards Sawyl and his men, setting out to avenge themselves on Cadog, are swallowed up in the ground!) Later, Cadog blesses the twelve who have done the shaving, and declares that:

> If judgement and useful counsel should be wanting in the whole of this country, let it be found here with you. If twelve wise ordained men should be wanting, let the counsel of twelve unordained clerics prevail. And if twelve clerics shall not be present, let judgement and counsel be allowed to twelve small boys and girls with unmarried women.

We are in the realm of Christianized fairy-tale. The shaving incident recalls the vindictive Nisien's maiming of the horses of the Irish king in the *Mabinogi* tale of 'Branwen': but here it is given Christian colouring by the number of the shavers, twelve, 'who figure in type the number of the twelve Apostles'. The tale has all the unsophisticated magic and coarse humour that appealed to Welsh audiences before Norman influence introduced more refined, romantic tastes. It seems improbable that twelve children would ever have held court at Llancarfan: real claims are embedded in an entertaining story, just as we still use stories and fables to bring home morals to children today.

There was one court which ultimately everyone had to attend: the terrible Day of Judgement. Just as friends in high places could help those charged with crimes on earth, so the Last Judgement could be faced with greater equanimity by those who knew they would rise from the dead under the protection of those in special favour with God. Laymen (at least, those powerful enough to have any choice in the matter) coveted burial in cemeteries where influential saints were buried. Rome was the most desirable burial-place of all, for there one could be buried in the company of St Peter, holder of the keys of Heaven, and several Welsh kings and bishops went on pilgrimage to Rome at the end of their days, to die and be buried there. But the Welsh churches could offer attractive alternative burial-places; and it was in their own interest to do so, for they gained valuable gifts in return for burial and commemoration of the laity. *The Life of St*

David claims that the site for David's monastery was chosen on the basis of an angelic prophecy that, of the believers buried there, 'scarcely one of them will pay the penalties of hell' (ch. 14). An angel promises St Cadog very special powers of intercession:

> The Lord thy God will free thy castle full of the souls of men, three times, in the Day of Judgement from eternal penalties. And as many ringlets or tufts as are joined together in thy cloak . . . so many persons shall be snatched for thy sake from perpetual penalties. Also every Saturday from this night for ever, let one soul be freed from infernal torments for thy love, and all your familiar friends, who shall have died in this place [i.e. all the members of the community of St Cadog, buried at Llancarfan] will be liberated from the sufferings of hell (para. 17).

Llancarfan, according to Cadog's biographer, had the right to bury all the people of Gwynlliog—or at least all the desirable people: exiles and women dying in childbirth were to be left for the cemetery of St Gwynllyw's church (para. 54). Doubtless the clergy of St Gwynllyw's church (now St Woolo's, Newport, Gwent) had their own views on this!

One can understand why, when a writer wanted to demonstrate St Padarn's magnanimity, he made the saint promise the repentant sinner, Eithir map Arthat, 'in the cemetery of this place [i.e. Llanbadarn] shalt thou be honourably buried. To thee a solemnity will be celebrated for ever by this company' (para. 31). Such promises must have been one of the strongest incentives to the laity to stay on the right side of the church. Then, like the Iorwert and Ruallaun remembered on a Breconshire stone monument,[14] when their lives were ended they could 'await in peace the dreadful coming of the Judgement', confident that their bodies were interred in sacred ground, their names preserved in lettering on stone, their souls' survival prayed for by the professional religious.

The sanctity of the saints not only rubbed off on to the

cemeteries where they were buried: it came to be believed that all objects connected with them, including their physical remains, had special powers. Relics were most important in attracting devotion, for they met the need for a religion to be keyed in to reality—as paganism was rooted in such basic objects as the sun and moon, water, trees, and stones. 'Seeing is believing': and relics, or at least the shrines by which they were protected, could be seen and wondered at.

The Celtic Church honoured a whole range of church possessions—altars, bells, staffs, Gospel books—on the grounds that they had once belonged to saints. The saints' *Lives* are full of stories purporting to explain the origin of the relics kept by the churches in whose interests the *Lives* were written. Occasionally the connection may have been genuine; but one can imagine how easily speculation would turn any ancient object kept in a church into 'St X's bell' or 'St X's staff', just as a somewhat improbable number of stately homes in England boast a bed slept in by Henry VIII.

Some at least of the venerated altars may have been portable ones—the type carried round by bishops and priests as they travelled to minister to their scattered flocks. In Britain surviving pre-Norman portable altars are uncommon, but one of stone was found in a grave at Ardwall Isle in North Britain; and a wooden altar, later encased in silver, was recovered from the coffin of the seventh-century Northumbrian saint, Cuthbert, when the coffin was opened early in the nineteenth century: it is now in the Library of the Dean and Chapter at Durham. St David was said to have been given an altar when he, with Teilo and Padarn, received gifts from the Patriarch of Jerusalem: several saints' *Lives* repeat this story, the *Life of St Teilo* (para. 9. ii) adding the attractive reason that David celebrated Mass more cheerfully than his companions! Though the story, in its present form, shows the influence of the Crusades, we need not doubt that it was meant to apply to an actual altar kept at St David's, which was, Rhigyfarch tells us, 'potent with many miracles'. Apparently too holy to be seen, the altar was 'concealed by coverings of skins' (*Life of St David*, ch. 48). Another church which claimed to possess a miraculous altar was that at Loyngarth in the Gower. The *Life of*

St Illtud tells how the body of a holy man was conveyed across the sea to St Illtud for burial, with an altar miraculously suspended above it. After the burial, the altar continued to hover above the grave, and 'numerous miracles were performed on account of its sanctity' (para. 22). This is a simpler version of a story about the altar told three centuries earlier by Nennius. Nennius provides examples of the miracles, including an account of how someone who ingeniously tested the altar by drawing a rod beneath it died within a month. Such punishment need be no more than coincidence; but such coincidences were the food on which miracle-tales were nourished.

Giraldus Cambrensis, in his *Itinerary*, declared that in Ireland, Scotland, and Wales, people were more frightened of swearing falsely by a bell than by the Gospels. The Celtic reverence for bells was unusual. In the Western Church as a whole, the attitude towards them was far more utilitarian: they were used to summon worshippers, but not until the tenth century was it felt that they warranted consecration as sacred objects. The Celtic bells were handbells, with a loop or handle at the top. Normally they had no clappers: like modern triangles, they would be struck with a separate piece of metal. The usual method of construction was to rivet together two sheets of copper, and then dip the bell into molten bronze. A brazen or cast bell is mentioned in the *Life of St Illtud* (para. 19), and a bell with a clapper in the *Life of St Cadog* (para. 27), but these could be anachronisms introduced by writers familiar with later bells, rather than true descriptions of the bells preserved at Llantwit and Llancarfan. Eight pre-Norman Welsh bells survive, six in Wales, two in Herefordshire. Most are very plain, but that from St Gwynhoedl's church at Llangwnadl, Caernarvonshire, has a beast's head worked at each end of its loop-handle. The bells would have been valuable objects, at a time when metalwork was a special skill, reserved for weapons and brooches and other prestigious objects. Just the quality of the metal, especially its colour, made a bell beautiful. In the *Life of St Cadog*, we hear of 'a certain most beautiful mottled bell', supposedly made by the renowned Gildas, and coveted by Cadog because 'the beauty and the sound and the colour had pleased him' (para. 27). We do not hear of bells made of what to us are precious metals; but the *Life of St Oudoceus* mentions a yellow bell kept at Llandaff which had the appearance of pure gold: to explain its unusual colour, it was said that the saint had fashioned it out of butter (para. 4).

The Celts often gave names to precious objects—swords, shields, etc.—which the craftsman had endowed with a distinctive character (rather as we name boats and houses). Giraldus Cambrensis, in his *Itinerary*, referred to the miraculous powers of a bell called 'Bangu', kept at Glascwm. The staff which was believed to have belonged to St Padarn was called 'Cyrwen', 'the holy staff with the crooked head'.[15] Staffs, the symbols of pastoral care, were made of wood, but surviving Irish examples show that the more honoured staffs might have their heads enshrined in metal, and their shafts ornamented with metal bands. When we read in the *Life of St Tatheus* (para. 10) that a staff was made from a golden fetter, it is presumably these trimmings that are meant. Padarn's staff was his share in the story of the gifts given to Padarn, David, and Teilo by the Patriarch of Jerusalem—though, in the version of the story in the *Life of St David*, David has appropriated all the gifts for himself (para. 48). There seems to have been a firm tradition about the gift of Padarn's staff (whether or not gifts to David and Teilo figured in the same tale), for one of the earliest-known examples of written Welsh verse celebrates 'Cyrwen. A wonderful gift', with which 'No other relic can be compared'.[16] This is a sophisticated verse, conforming to the strict bardic conventions of metre and alliteration—the sort of poetry with which the native princes were entertained. Presumably it was composed for the high-born clergy at Llanbadarn. It reminds us that the saints and their relics would have been celebrated in Welsh, as well as in Latin, though for a long time the church did not consider compositions in the native tongue worthy of record, so that it is the Latin *Lives* of the saints that survive today.[17]

Manuscripts were costly, and not to be squandered on unworthy material. Of all manuscripts, copies of the Gospels were most precious, not just for the labour and resources spent on them, but because they contained the word of God. Like magicians' spells, the words, quite apart from their meaning, were imbued with power. Ascetics recited the Psalms to keep devils at bay; Cassiodorus (founder of the monastery at Vivarium in Italy where manuscripts were collected and copied) declared that every word of the Lord written by a scribe was a wound inflicted upon Satan. Their potency made Gospel books an ideal place for agreements subject to divine sanction to be recorded; and the grants of land and other agreements written in the late eighth or ninth century in the spare spaces in the Gospels of St Chad (the *Book of Lichfield*) show that this practice was of early origin in Wales. Who would dare violate these agreements, when the God who was invoked to witness them was made manifest in the pages on which they were copied?

Perhaps the most common way for the ordinary people to enlist the aid of the saints was through holy wells. These were believed to owe their origins to the saints: St Cybi struck his staff on a rock, and water gushed forth (*Life of St Cybi*, para. 15); the water of St Gwenfrewi's well sprang up from the ground stained with blood from the severance of her head (*Life of St Winifred*, para. 14). There were biblical precedents for these tales, such as the story of Aaron striking a rock in the desert, whereupon water flowed. The healing properties and other miraculous powers claimed for the wells would in some cases have had a rational basis, in some special quality of their water. We are told that it was St David who made the water at Bath health-giving and warm (*Life of St David*, para. 13)!

Today, the best-preserved wells are those which continued to attract pilgrims until recent times; sometimes shelters have been erected over the well, steps built by which bathers could enter the water, and niches provided where offerings to the saint could be placed. At Holywell in Flintshire, the well named after St Winifred is housed in an elaborate medieval structure: this healing well was once counted as one of the Seven Wonders of Wales, and it still attracts sufferers in search of cure. A less sophisticated atmosphere surrounds St Cybi's well at Llangybi, Caernarvonshire. Beyond the churchyard, a path leads down through the fields to a little stream at the foot of a hill. It leads to a group of ruined buildings, roughly built of stone. To the right is a cottage, provided for the guardian of the well in the eighteenth century. This is built up against an older building of huge boulders, which encloses the main pool;[18] a second pool is hidden away to the rear. The use of mortar in the building housing the pool makes a twelfth-century or later date probable, but the structure is certainly archaic in style, with its massive masonry and its rounded corners and inward-sloping walls—originally it seems the building had a stone corbelled roof, that is, the roof was formed by placing each layer of stones a little further inwards.

St Seiriol's well at Penmon also underwent modernization in the eighteenth century: there, the building housing the pool provides not only a ledge on which visitors could stand and niches for their offerings, but stone seats for those waiting to bathe, or simply enjoying the chance to sit and chat. At St Non's well, near St David's, there were also benches beside the well. The remains of a chapel stand alongside, and a seventh- or eighth-century cross-inscribed stone incorporated in the masonry shows that the site was in early use.

Veneration for the bodily remains of persons of special sanctity received a powerful stimulus when, in the eighth century, the remains of the early saints and martyrs at Rome were divided up and dispersed. But the cult of relics seems already to have spread to the Celtic churches from the Mediterranean world, probably mainly by way of Gaul, along the same routes as monasticism. Most of our evidence comes from Ireland, where open-air 'slab shrines', made to house disinterred remains, are found, thought to be of sixth- or seventh-century date. In North Britain, an altar found in the oratory at Ardwall Isle contained a little cavity or *fossa* for relics. By the seventh or eighth century, Armagh in Ireland claimed to possess relics of Roman as well as native saints, and even 'a relic of the blood of Christ'.[19] But the Welsh Church was apparently less outward-looking than her Irish cousin: she lacked the links with the continental Church which Ireland enjoyed through the many scholars and monks who had left her shores for voluntary exile overseas, and she held out far longer than the Irish Church against the pressure to conform to Roman usages, including the Roman Easter date. When, in the late-eleventh- and twelfth-century *Lives* of the Welsh saints, we at last find evidence for the importance of relics in the life of the Celtic Church in Wales, the relics referred to are those of the native saints.

Indeed, there are signs that in Wales itself the cult of bodily relics may have been slow to take root (either that, or it had suffered severe setbacks with the destruction of churches and their relics during long centuries of raiding and warfare). The authors of the earlier *Lives* (around the turn of the century) do not seem to know what has happened to the relics of their heroes. Sometimes their place of burial is mentioned—David is allegedly buried 'in the grounds of his own monastery' (*Life of St David*, ch. 65)—but references to shrines housing their bones, or miracles effected by them, are either confined to the later *Lives*, or are given a foreign setting. Thus the *Life of St Padarn* accepts the claim of the Breton church, Vannes, to possess the remains of St Paternus; while the earliest version of the *Life of St Cadog* sends Cadog to a monastery in Sicily to die—a monastery that had recently been in the news because the Pope had been imprisoned there while campaigning against the Normans in Sicily. St Illtud, whom early tradition, as expressed in the *Life of St Samson*, seemed happy to regard as buried at his own monastery (Llantwit), is in his twelfth-century *Life* said to be buried in Brittany, at Dol.

The Normans were accustomed to the elaborate cult of relics as practised within the Roman Church. It seems that when the Normans arrived in Wales, some Welsh churches, embarrassed at being unable to display their saints' remains, yet determined to show that these remains existed and were as miraculous as those of continental saints, solved the dilemma by claiming that their saints' relics were preserved abroad. The earliest version of the *Life of St Cadog* is careful to explain why the relics of Cadog have not been brought back from Sicily to Llancarfan: no Briton is allowed to enter the basilica over his tomb, lest 'a Briton . . . from Llancarfan . . . shall at some time by the theft of the relics of his body carry away from there the sacred soil and . . . cause all the miracles and all the grace of that saint to depart . . . to his own land' (para. 39).

When Urban, the bishop of Glamorgan, established his see at

Llandaff in the early twelfth century, he sought to win the support of the Normans in consolidating and extending his position in the Welsh Church. He founded a cathedral, to be built in the grand Norman manner: and in Norman-approved fashion he dedicated this to St Peter, as well as to three native saints, Dubricius, Teilo, and Oudoceus. The site of Llandaff seems to have been chosen because the Normans had established a stronghold there; we have no evidence that any of the three saints who were now claimed to have been the first three bishops of Llandaff had previously been associated with the site—indeed, Teilo and Dubricius seem to have been selected because their foundations were grouped in Ystrad Tywi and Archenfield respectively, the areas to the west and east of Glamorgan which Llandaff was attempting (vainly) to include in her diocese. The grandiose new cathedral would not have been complete without the shrines of its patron saints. The *Book of Llandaff* (a compilation of the material used by Llandaff to support its claims to be an ancient and orthodox see, with an extensive territorial diocese) includes the *Lives* of the three supposed founder-saints, written in Llandaff's interest; and, of these, the *Life of St Dubricius* includes a detailed account of how the saint's relics were translated to Llandaff from his grave on Bardsey Island (paras. 8–9). The authenticity of the bones was proved beyond all doubt, for when they were washed the water used came to the boil! One can only hope that the memory of which of the thousands of saints buried on Bardsey was Dubricius was more reliable than the memory of the date of his death, for the combination of day and date given for Dubricius's decease in the *Book of Llandaff* is an impossible one—the fourteenth of November would not have fallen on a Sunday in A.D. 612, as is claimed.

Perhaps this translation in A.D. 1120 set the fashion for other churches to recover the remains of their founders. The *Life of St Gwynllyw*, which is influenced by Llandaff's claims, says that Gwynllyw was buried under the floor of his church, 'where a frequent visitation of angels was seen about the place of his burial, and sick people with divers disorders were made well from every ill' (para. 10). When chapters were added to the *Life of St Cadog*, telling of miracles wrought by the saint after his death, these mentioned without comment that Llancarfan possessed the saint's remains (paras. 40 and 44). The complications that could arise when churches revived or invented claims to possess the bodies of their founders is amusingly illustrated by a story in Llandaff's *Life of St Teilo*. In claiming to possess St Teilo's relics, Llandaff found herself in competition with two other churches which believed they possessed his body—Penally, his family burial-place, and Llandeilo Fawr, St Teilo's chief founda-tion. Llandaff's propagandists explained away the embarrassing surfeit of bodies in characteristically ingenious fashion. According to the *Life of St Teilo*, immediately Teilo died the three churches put forward their claims to the right to take his body. After a night spent in prayer and fasting, behold! the claimants discovered that there was no longer just one body, but one each (para. 9). Of course, in Llandaff's opinion, the location of the real body was not in doubt—miracles at his tomb in Llandaff show that the real Teilo is there. But a marginal note in the *Book of Llandaff* is probably nearer the truth when it says Llandeilo is Teilo's place of burial: and in the *Life of St Oudoceus* (para. 1) Oudoceus is said to have taken some relics of Teilo from there.

Relics provided a tangible link with the supernatural. Through them the saints exercised the powers vested in them by God. Often the so-called miracles effected by altars or wells or bones would just be happenings inexplicable in the current state of knowledge—the curing of psychosomatic ailments, for example. But they were sufficient to impress people and to attract pilgrims, whether these came to venerate, or to seek a miracle for them-selves. A story in the *Life of St Cadog* (para. 36) illustrates what could happen. It concerns 'a certain foolish rustic', who dared to look on the tombs of St Cadog's disciples in a Scottish church, which none save virgins and the clergy were allowed to see. His punishment is frightful: the rustic's eye bursts open, and the eyeball drops out, hanging suspended by the optic nerve. From that time on the rustic travels from place to place, and 'Many used to bestow a reward on him, that he might show them the rent orb of the eye. Therefrom his compatriots were learning to fear God more and more, and reverently to glorify him with his saint.' This sort of miracle—perhaps really an accidental injury—was custom-made to satisfy man's perennial hunger for the horrific and the marvellous, the hunger that horror films satisfy today.

Oaths were sworn on relics, as we still swear on the Bible. According to the *Life of St Cadog*, the bell called 'Gildas's bell' kept at Llancarfan had been blessed by the Pope, with the instruction 'that thereon every principal oath be made . . . And if anyone shall perjure himself thereon, unless he have done due penance, he shall without doubt be anathema here and hereafter' (para. 27). Respect for the relics was an important factor in enforcing justice. An amusing story in the *Life of St Cadog* describes the impact of relics on a stupid peasant who is refusing to admit that he has stolen an ox. One of the officials of Llancarfan arrives at the court bearing a sacred Gospel book. But it is not the Gospel that brings the rustic to confess: the cleric went up to him, 'and suddenly for a joke bared his knife of no small size, and brandishing it with shaking hand said "O stupid, here is the knife of saint Cadog. If thou perjure thyself thereon, thou shalt die the death at once, because it will penetrate thine entrails" ' (para. 33). Terrified, the rustic threw himself at the cleric's feet, confessing his guilt. The use of relics in legal proceedings was a valuable source of income for the church: as a result of the rustic's confession, not only did the king and others present at the court make an offering to the Gospel book, but they made a gift to the cleric, and handed over the convicted thief to serve Llancarfan as a slave.

Oaths were also taken on relics to pledge the swearer to a certain action—to keep the peace, for instance, or to honour a grant of land. As early as the sixth century we hear from Gildas of princes confirming their oaths at the altar. Much later, we are told that at a church in Scotland dedicated to St Cadog, kings and other dignitaries would, 'if by chance a matter of great dissension has arisen among them', take an oath on the tombs of Cadog's disciples, and 'If any one breaks that oath, he will go down to death before the end of that year' (*Life of St Cadog*, para. 36). St Padarn's staff had a similar peace-making role: 'For so great is the

III LATE EXAMPLES
OF CELTIC
ECCLESIASTICAL
STONE-CARVING

(a) The font at Newborough
Anglesey (*left*)

(b) The monument at
Llanfihangel-y-traethau
commemorating the
mother of the church's
twelfth-century founder

IV HOLY WELLS

(a) The well at Partrishow, with niches for offerings (*left*)
(b) A corner of the well at Llangybi, Caerns., showing the surrounding ledge to accommodate pilgrims, and the steps by which sufferers seeking cure could enter

service of that staff, that, if any two are in discord, they are made to agree by swearing together on it' (*Life of St Padarn*, para. 11).

The relics were the clergy's credentials when they toured to collect tribute or enforce the law. Their powers were also used to protect the churches and their rights. We have seen that gifts of land to the Church might be recorded in Gospel books; another way in which relics could be used to confirm church ownership of property is described in a charter appended to the *Life of St Cadog* (para. 55). The previous owners of some land acquired by Llancarfan were met by the clergy, who 'brought the cross of saint Cadog and his earth, and going round the aforesaid land . . . claimed it, and scattered the earth of the aforesaid saint upon it in the presence of suitable witnesses in token of permanent possession.' Many stories in the saints' *Lives* tell how the miraculous powers of relics protect the saints' churches from attack, or enforce restitution.

However, the relics would be no defence against pagan or sacrilegious enemies. Sometimes the relics were the main motive for raids, either because of their intrinsic value and that of the shrines in which they might be housed, or because to steal them would have the same demoralizing effect on the neighbourhood where they were revered as the seizure of an army's standard. In the *Life of St Illtud*, we hear how an English army returned from a raid on Glamorgan with the bell of St Illtud 'tied about the neck of one particular horse, which . . . took the lead' (para. 25). But their battle trophy proved elusive: miraculously the horse turned back towards Glamorgan, and returned the bell to St Illtud's church.

In times of danger, the church not only supported the people's morale, but offered practical help. Fugitives were given sanctuary within the religious enclosures, whether they were individuals fleeing from justice, or the neighbouring populace hoping to escape harm during an enemy attack. Of course, the sanctuary was not always honoured, especially during times of political unrest; and in the late eleventh and twelfth centuries we find Llancarfan anxiously defending its rights to grant refuge. The

Life of St Cadog includes a whole series of miracle stories (paras. 22–5) designed to show that Llancarfan possesses written confirmation of its right to give sanctuary; supposedly King Arthur originally conferred this right, and it was subsequently confirmed by other eminent kings. The sanctuary was to last for seven years, seven months, and seven days. A later addition to the *Life* (para. 69) elaborates on the terms of refuge: anyone who has slain a fugitive who has taken refuge in Cadog's land of Gwynlliog 'will pay one hundred cows according to judgement'. When the period of sanctuary was expired, the fugitive was allowed to stay for one night within the bounds of Gwynlliog, but after that he must leave Gwynlliog for 'whatever other place of security he might wish'. St Cadog's right to give sanctuary within Gwynlliog was to be 'like to the refuge of saint David in Vallis Rosina'; but according to a late version of the *Life of St David*,[20] St David's rights of refuge extended well beyond the 'Vallis Rosina' (the valley where his monastery was set). Refuge was to be granted to fugitives wherever there was an enclosure dedicated to David, and his sanctuary was to take precedence over that of any other king or chieftain or bishop or saint. This is the sort of claim that enabled St David's to build up a huge territorial diocese for itself, as under Norman influence the structure of the Welsh Church conformed to the Roman diocesan pattern. David was an influential saint, with many dedications, and almost all the foundations dedicated to him were swallowed up in the medieval diocese of St David's, except for a few outliers in Archenfield, which fell into the control of Hereford.

The churches would not expect to harbour fugitives without reward. An addition to the *Life of St Cadog* (para. 50) tells of a special official, the *sepeliarius*, literally 'grave-digger'. Apparently he was the caretaker of the graveyard, with duties that included the custody of sacred remains, for with three messengers he had the job of 'serv[ing] the clergy with the relics'. These men did not have a full share in the income that was divided between the clergy, 'But persons, who arrived at the church for sanctuary, and returned from sanctuary, gave them their honour-price, to wit, a ewe with lamb or four pence.' (It was the *sepeliarius* who had taken the Gospel book to the court where a peasant was being tried for the theft of an ox, and had forced a confession by brandishing his knife at the thief.[21])

In times of war, the custom of sheltering refugees and their possessions—whether from the churches' own lands, or from the neighbouring area as a whole—greatly increased the attractiveness to raiders of religious sites. Precious shrines and other church treasures would sometimes be the motive for attack; but not all churches had much of value, especially after centuries of looting, and what they had might well be hidden, as we hear that St Cadog's relics were sent into hiding at the monastery of Mammelliat when the Llancarfan community heard of the approach of the English army (*Life of St Cadog*, para. 40). But the stock and stores of grain from church lands could not be easily hidden, and these and the possessions of the local people could only be entrusted to the safe-keeping of the church enclosure. The *Life of St Gwynllyw* relates how Earl Harold's army broke into Gwynllyw's church, and found it 'full of garments and provisions and many precious things', for the local people, hearing of Harold's invasion of Glamorgan, 'took their goods to the sanctuaries of the saints' before hiding themselves in the woods. Only when some stolen cheeses were miraculously found to be bloody inside did the army restore their booty to the church—but their transgression was not forgiven, for as the hagiographer tells us, 'in the next month for that iniquity and other transgressions [Harold] was conquered in the battle of Hastings' (para. 13).

When the local people, as well as their goods, took refuge in the religious enclosures, these could become the rallying-points of defence. In the *Life of St Illtud* we are told that, hearing of a Welsh attack on Norman-occupied Glamorgan, 'the clergy of saint Illtud with the inhabitants of their district . . . fortified themselves by means of a ditch . . . endeavouring to protect their wealth by defence' (para. 26).

———————

By the simpler folk in particular, the efficacy of Christianity would be judged by such basic matters as the fertility of men and crops, freedom from sickness, or success in war. The conception may seem primitive; but we still celebrate harvest festival in

87

thanksgiving for the year's crops. It must have been this sort of concern that motivated most of the visitors and pilgrims to religious sites: the sick to beg for cure, owners of stock to pray for the health of their cattle, princes to pray for success in war. The saints' *Lives*, especially the south-eastern *Lives* with their accent on the efficacy of the saints' relics, may well have been designed to attract pilgrims, as well as to defend the rights of the foundations in whose interests they were written. The two motives were indeed connected, for if a shrine could gain the respect of the Normans for its sanctity, it would be safer from their interference. St David's early safeguarded its position by attracting in A.D. 1081 no less a pilgrim than William the Conqueror. The detailed localization of the miracle stories in many of the saints' *Lives* gives them the character of guidebooks designed to reveal what places were to be venerated by pilgrims. When we find that two late versions of the *Life of St David* (the Vespasian recension of Rhigyfarch's *Life*, and the version edited by Giraldus Cambrensis) provide additional localizations for incidents, but differ in the place-names supplied, we can see that the writers were not following any firm tradition when they identified the places where things happened: they had another motive. St David's and some other influential shrines—Bardsey Island, St Winifred's Well, and St Beuno's church at Clynnog Fawr among them—succeeded in attracting Norman as well as Welsh pilgrims, and were important pilgrimage centres in medieval times.

5

Church Economy

As soon as clergy and monks devoted themselves to religion full-time, the Church needed the means to support them; and if it was to achieve any degree of freedom from dependence on laymen, it needed to acquire its own land. The monks whose life is described in the monastic rule section of the *Life of St David* were able to shun all gifts only because they owned land from which they could glean a living.

Some early Christian settlements may have been sited on virgin territory, where, provided the local ruler proved amenable, the settlers would be able to appropriate whatever land they might need. Even allowing for the vast areas of grazing needed by the Welsh pastoralists, there must have been wide tracts of little-used land in pre-Norman Wales. The numerous early churches sited in once-wooded valleys, for instance, suggest that the founders carved out settlement sites for themselves from the inhospitable forests. Centuries later, their appropriation of such wildernesses brought the churches into dispute with the Normans, to judge from a story in the *Life of St Illtud*. The Normans revelled in wild forests and valleys, where in the lull between bouts of fighting they could stir their blood with the excitement of the chase, and eventually large areas of Britain were declared Royal Forests, where only the King was allowed to hunt. When in the twelfth century Illtud's biographer represented the local king, Meirchion, as incensed against the saint, because in settling at Hodnant 'he had occupied the waste, which in his judgement was more fit for hunting' (para. 8), this surely reflected a dispute in the writer's own time—an attempted or actual seizure of church land for use as a hunting reserve.

Other land was given to the Church, either to found or to increase the holdings of a religious settlement. The position was complicated because most land was the joint possession of the kin-group, while individually owned land was subject to set laws of inheritance. Perhaps 'The small waste plot . . . [which] Occon, son of Asaitgen, gave to Madomnuac', a donation recorded on a cross-inscribed stone at Llanllyr, Cardiganshire,[1] was land Occon's heirs would be quite happy to relinquish. We have seen that sometimes an entire kin-group may have participated in the foundation of a monastery, handing over their lands to the Church. Some would lead a communal religious life; others would live with their families and work their lands much as before, except that they would now be tenants of the Church. Similarly, when a gift of land was made to the Church, this might mean simply that the kin who farmed it became tenants of the Church instead of clients of a secular ruler: thus one of the charters appended to the *Life of St Cadog* records that 'Gualluuir gave to God and to saint Cadog the land of Pencarnov for his soul for ever . . . [He] also willed this township to Iudnou his son, that he and his heirs might serve the familia of Cadog with the produce of this land in addition to themselves' (para. 59). Some of these charters specify the rents to be paid to the Church by tenants: normally these comprise beer, bread, meat, and sometimes honey. Subject churches were required to pay similar rents to their mother churches: Cadog's disciple Elli is said to have made his foundations subject to Llancarfan, and to have provided an annual *pensio* to Llancarfan of 'provisions for three nights in the summer and as many in the winter' (para. 63). The tenants benefited not only from the ministry and protection of the Church, and the chance to have some of their children educated by the monks and clergy, but also from freedom from liability to pay tribute and other services to secular lords.

Donors of land to the Church had much to gain. In a society where high status was dependent on magnanimous giving, donations of land to the Church provided a splendid opportunity for display of generosity. They also ensured that the donor's soul would be remembered and prayed for by the Church. St Cadog was said to have promised the kingdom of heaven 'to all who should increase the possessions of [a certain church] with lands or monies or alms' (para. 58); while the canons of Llantwit were supported by farmsteads 'given by the people to keep in memory their souls' (*Life of St Illtud*, para. 12). Sometimes, too, gifts of land must have served as peace offerings, to compensate the Church for offences against it. This is the situation frequently pictured by the hagiographers: in a chapter appended to the *Life of St Padarn*, for instance (para. 31), a prince whose followers have slain one of Padarn's servants goes to beg pardon of the saint, and promises: 'that I may make thy mind placable towards me, I will dedicate to thee part of my finest land without reclaiming of tribute of any person.'

The major churches in particular found themselves with lands far in excess of what was needed for the religious communities' support, and far in excess of what the monks and clergy could work themselves, even had they been willing to do so. To refuse land would be to undermine the carefully nurtured relationship between laymen and the Church. Besides, a use could always be found for extra income; and it would be unrealistic to suppose that the average abbot was any less prone to acquisitiveness than other men. By the late eleventh century, the picture that emerges of the major foundations in south-east Wales—Llancarfan and Llantwit in particular—is of wealthy, property-owning concerns, engrossed in the management of their extensive estates. This picture may not be representative of the Welsh churches as a whole: the south-eastern coastal plain is one of the most fertile areas of Wales, where agriculture could prove most profitable; it was fertile too in foreign contacts, so that social and economic change was probably here in advance of the rest of the country; and the saints' *Lives* and charters which are our chief sources are naturally preoccupied with land-ownership, since they date from or were revised at the time when the Normans were appropriating much church property. There were still ascetics within the Church, who chose to live by their own labour: Giraldus Cambrensis praises those on Priestholm. Nevertheless, one doubts whether the picture is wholly misleading. History can furnish all too many parallels of religious institutions which went through the same stages: success brought wealth, wealth entailed worldliness.

One way in which land-ownership could prove a tax on the

clergy's time and energy was by drawing the church into litigation. Ownership of property and the definition of boundaries were as always fruitful sources of dispute. The *Life of St Gwynllyw* relates how 'A certain layman unjustly laid a claim to a portion of land which the clergy of the most blessed Gwynllyw held of right.' A day was fixed for the case to be heard, and with a little help from St Gwynllyw—who enabled him to cross an unfordable river without realizing it—the church's deacon attended the court and 'snatched the disputed land from lay hands' (para. 16).

Some of the cross-incribed stone monuments served to mark the boundaries of church lands. But the Church's most powerful weapon in defending its possessions was literacy. As we have seen, by the eighth century at least gifts to the Church were being recorded in Gospel books, and their inviolability guaranteed by divine sanctions. In south-east Wales, we occasionally find land grants recorded on stone. At Ogmore, Glamorgan, an eleventh-century inscription proclaimed: 'Be it known to all that Arthmail has given a piece of land to God and to Glywys and to Nertat and to Fili the bishop.'[2] The wording imitates that used in contemporary charters, and a damaged inscription of similar date on a cross-slab from Merthyr Mawr, Glamorgan,[3] refers specifically to a *grefium*, a written deed of the type used to record grants of land. To have a grant recorded in writing, with all the attendant ceremonial of formal witnessing and so forth, would pander to the donor's sense of importance, as well as safeguarding the Church's right to possession. To record the grant on stone not only gave it the greatest possible degree of permanence, but created a monument to the donor's generosity which would stand for all to see.

The details of early Welsh economy are still a matter for debate. The old view was that the Celts were wandering pastoralists, but it is now recognized that arable land as well as stock was important. Not only did the bondsmen or unfree tenants, tied for life to their village, grow grain to provide bread for their lords and fodder for their lords' horses, but the Welsh Laws show that free tenants also paid part of their rent in grain. Crop-growing is frequently mentioned in those saints' *Lives* which relate to the churches on the fertile south-eastern coastal plain. St Illtud is said to have miraculously freed Llantwit's land of flooding, so that it 'was fertile for agriculture, and what was not arable, the clergy had in meadow and fodder abundance for cattle' (*Life of St Illtud*, para. 13). But the *Life of St David*, from the much bleaker south-western extremity of Wales, also depicts the monks plough-ing the soil, and eating bread as the main part of their diet (chs. 22, 24). In the *Lives* of St Brynach and of St Cadog, wheaten bread is mentioned; Illtud's *Life* refers to bread made from bar-ley.

The diet of the Celtic churchmen would seem both unexciting and, often, nutritionally inadequate to us. But only occasionally is this a sign of deliberate self-denial: their lay contemporaries, too, enjoyed a restricted diet, dependent as they were on themselves supplying all or almost all their dietary needs. Those ascetics who did seek to subdue the flesh by adopting a still sparser diet were pushed to extremes. The monastic rule section of the *Life of St David* stipulates that, after a long day's toil, 'Every one restores and refreshes his weary limbs by partaking of supper, not, how-ever, to excess, for too much, though it be of bread alone, engen-ders self-indulgence' (ch. 24). Bread and herbs seasoned with salt, with water to drink, was to be the diet of all except those for whom age, illness, or long travel made richer sustenance essential. Herbs, or wild plants, must have been an important element in the diet of the Celts, providing much-needed vitamins: an amaz-ing variety of plants can be eaten (and were, until very recent times), from nettles to elderflowers, from wild cresses to the dandelion.

Although most of the hagiographers were keen to claim that their saints had led ascetic lives, eating only bread, and perhaps fish, and some sort of drink, Gildas's reference to clergy so fat that the excess of flesh made their voices hoarse shows that this self-denial was not the norm in the sixth-century Church. Besides, the hagiographers let slip references that show that a far more varied diet was enjoyed by many monks and clergy, at least at the time when they were writing. They mention pigs, cattle, and sheep being kept on church estates to provide meat. Sometimes wild animals—stags, and winged game—figured on the menu. A verse incorporated in paragraph 20 of the *Life of St Cadog* visualizes the saint's successors enjoying a luxurious diet:

> Boar's flesh will sustain,
>   easy to hunters for the seeking;
> Sweetness of honey
>   will provide entertainment for the clergy
> A table of winged game caught by a comely foe
> Our wholesome fare will be, not sickly, therefore free from
>   sickness.

Freedom to hunt and hawk was an aristocratic privilege, forbidden in Welsh law to bondsmen. In following this pursuit, the clergy were clinging to the way of life in which most of them had been brought up, the life of the secular nobility with their hunting and feasting. In the ninth century the Welsh tribute to the English king Athelstan included hunting dogs and hawks.

Dairy produce was a staple food. A single cow could provide a cleric or anchorite with most of his dietary needs for much of the year. Indeed, St Tatheus and his seven disciples are said to have been provided with food 'through summer and autumn' (i.e. after calving) by a cow given him in payment for teaching one of his pupils (*Life of St Tatheus*, para. 7). Some men from King Rhun's army are said to have gone to St Cadog's estates to demand a drink of milk, ' "for milk abounds there always" ' (*Life of St Cadog*, para. 24). Cheeses were among the goods placed for safekeeping in St Gwynllyw's church in the eleventh century (para. 13). Those calves that were not destined to become milkproducers in their turn would provide meat, as well as hides to make clothes and bags and other leather goods; monasteries and churches where manuscripts were produced needed a plentiful supply of calf-skins for making vellum.

For those who favoured some less abstemious drink than water, there was mead, or beer, and perhaps sometimes wine. Beer, honey, meat, and bread were the staple components of the food rents specified in the charters appended to the *Life of St Cadog*. Wine was, of course, needed for sacramental use: an incident in the *Life of St David* (ch. 33) draws attention to the problems encountered in obtaining it. A spring has gushed forth at the saint's prayer, 'and since that region produced no vines, the water was turned into wine for the celebrating of the sacrament of the Lord's Body.' The wine- and oil-jars imported into western Britain from the Eastern Mediterranean and Gaul in the fifth to seventh centuries probably contained oil and wine for sacramental, as well as for luxury use.

Honey for mead could be produced at home. But here too St David's seems to have run into difficulties. Rhigyfarch tells a touching story of how the bees from St David's followed David's disciple, Midunnauc, when he set out for Ireland—for he had looked after them. Three times he put out to sea: three times the bees flew after him. Eventually St David let them depart with his blessing, and prayed that they would increase in Ireland and abandon their former home. Rhigyfarch adds that this is the situation in his own day: Ireland abounds in honey, but swarms of bees brought to St David's 'have dwindled and faded away' (ch. 43). David's generosity in allowing the bees to depart would have been much admired by Rhigyfarch's audience—for according to Welsh tradition bees came from Paradise.

Apart from land and livestock, the Church accumulated wealth in the form of luxury goods—fine cloaks, spears, swords and so forth. These goods might seem inappropriate in an ecclesiastical context, but in the unspecialized Welsh economy they were among the few durable objects of value. In one of the charters appended to the *Life of St Cadog*, a foster-son of King Morcant gives one of Cadog's clerics 'his gilded sword, Hipiclaur, which had the worth of seventy cows' (para. 62). Immediately the sword is passed on to King Morcant, to obtain from him confirmation of the donation of some land to the Church. Works of craftsmanship like this sword were not collectors' pieces: they were currency.

Tithing became an important source of church revenue. It may have been introduced in the Celtic churches at an early date, in accordance with the requirements of Mosaic law,[4] but our evidence from Wales at least is late. Giraldus Cambrensis, writing in the late twelfth century, cites a tradition that tithing had been introduced into Britain by Germanus of Auxerre (the bishop who visited Britain to crush the Pelagian heresy): he says that the

Welsh 'give a tenth of all their property ... either when they marry, or go on a pilgrimage, or, by the counsel of the Church, are persuaded to amend their lives'.[5] Even a man with ten sons would hand over one to the church, like a 'rich and landed person' in the *Life of St Tatheus*, who, 'having ten sons, vowed to commend the tenth to the study of letters and to serve God' (para. 7). Chapters added to the *Life of St Cadog* specify how the tithe, together with bequests and payments on behalf of those taking sanctuary within the church are to be shared out among the clergy. One third of a person's tithe is to be paid to his confessor; one third to those who will offer prayers for him; one third to the altar, i.e. to be divided among the clergy who officiate at the church, of whom the abbot, *doctor* (teacher), and priest are to receive the major share (paras. 50–2).

The *claswyr* who divided church income between them were a far cry from the early monks at St David's, for whom 'All things are in common; there is no "mine" or "thine", for whosoever should say "my book" or "my anything else" would be straightway subjected to a severe penance' (*Life of St David*, ch. 28). The temptation to avarice that was inevitably placed in the way of the clergy once the Church accrued worldly wealth is illustrated by a story in the *Life of St Illtud* (para. 25). A herd of horses has fallen into the hands of the *claswyr* at Llantwit; but one horse is superior to all the rest, and who is to have this horse as his share? 'Wherefore each single one was saying, "That one will be mine", whilst another was answering, "I will not allow such a choice to be made." ... This contention persisted ... till the morrow, almost giving rise to the murder of many.' The problem was insoluble: eventually a miracle removed the difficulty by making every horse exactly the same.

Wealth was not something just to be stored away: this was a society where gift-giving played an important part in defining social relationships. To impress a prince with the magnificence of a sword you had managed to acquire, you presented it to him, and he would lose face if he could not give something equally generous in return. Perishable wealth (foodstuffs) was given away through hospitality and charity, which were social obligations, enforced by law, not casual open-handedness. It was by feasting their retainers that the princes kept their loyalty; to fail to dispense hospitality on a scale commensurate with one's status in society was to forfeit that status. The Church could find religious motives for its adherence to these native institutions, turning established custom into a Christian virtue. Gildas praised the British princes for their almsgiving; and in the *Life of St Tatheus* the hospitality offered to the saint and his disciples by a rich man in Gwent is explained in Christian terms: 'for he remembered the word of the Lord . . . "I was a stranger and ye took me in"' (para. 4).

The powerful abbots, like the princes, were judged by the number of their dependents and by the scale on which they entertained. At Llancarfan, St Cadog is boasted to have fed daily 'one hundred clergy, and one hundred soldiers and one hundred workmen, and one hundred poor persons, with the same number of widows. This was the number of his household, besides servants in attendance and esquires and strangers, also guests . . .' (para. 18). When some squires roughly demanded milk, Cadog's steward angrily refused them, astounded at their presumption: 'Are ye not without understanding, reckoning that at least our master is a man of great honour and dignity, since of a truth he owns a great household, three hundred men . . . besides children and women?' (para. 24). This is not a picture of a sixth-century abbot: the writer is visualizing St Cadog as the sort of powerful and influential abbot who came to hold sway at Llancarfan after centuries during which the Church's estates and responsibilities had steadily increased.

Though the Church was lavish in its hospitality, it rebelled against the concept of hospitality as an obligation, rather than a favour. Several saints' *Lives* tell similar stories, in which a prince tries to force hospitality from the Church, but is resisted by the saint. The saint is more than willing to provide hospitality, but only of his own volition. When the arch-villain Maelgwn orders St Brynach to prepare him supper, 'The saint, wishing that he and his and also his loca, [i.e.] *monasteries*, should be free from every suit, asserted that he owed no supper to the king, nor was he willing in any way to obey his unjust command' (*Life of St Brynach*, para. 11). But once a miracle has made the king repent

97

of his presumption, Brynach gladly offers him the night's entertainment he had previously refused. The point was that entertaining one's social superior was a form of tribute, a recognition of inferiority: St Cadog is said to have refused a demand for food 'owing to the harshness of the words, as though demanding tribute from a free man' (para. 3). The Church wanted to offer hospitality in the way that a prince offered entertainment to his clients, not like a client repaying a debt to his lord.

In Celtic society, the obligations of kinship ensured some degree of social welfare: orphans had aunts and uncles or grandparents to protect them; the aged had a home with their sons. Interestingly, in the *Lives* of the Welsh saints, I have been able to find no reference to the elderly among the needy people whom the saints are claimed to have helped. But there was still plenty of scope for the Church's charity: widows, especially young ones, may well have preferred a life within the Church to domination by their mothers or mothers-in-law, and their domestic skills, such as spinning and child-care, would have been welcomed by the clergy, who needed clothes for themselves and nurses for the small children entrusted to them for education. When St Cadog wanted a length of thread, he was said to have obtained it from 'a certain widow' (*Life of St Cadog*, para. 11). Strangers and outcasts were without provision in the social structure, and here the Church's charity was very much in need. St David is said to have fed 'a multitude of orphans, wards, widows, needy, sick, feeble, and pilgrims' (*Life of St David*, ch. 31). When St Illtud retreated to live as an anchorite in a cave by the river Ewenny, the poor and widows were said to have lamented: 'Who will be our protection? Who with overflowing heart will dispel our poverty? He gave bountifully' (*Life of St Illtud*, para. 19), while his wife Trinihid was said to have comforted 'innumerable widows and nuns and poor people in her charge' (para. 16).

When famine threatened, the Church's charity could mean the difference between life and death, for the Church's large estates enabled it to accumulate large stores of grain. St Cadog is said to have asked his teacher, Bachan, to allow him to share out a hidden supply of grain that had been miraculously revealed to him: for otherwise the words might be quoted against them: 'He who hides away corn is cursed among the peoples, but a blessing rests on the head of those who distribute it' (*Life of St Cadog*, para. 11).

Long after the Celtic Church had ceased to exist, Celtic-style hospitality was to persist within the Church in Wales. The feasting and entertainments continued within the abbots' halls. The Welsh poets found new patrons in the Cistercians; and when one of these poets, Tudur Aled, sought to praise his patron, the abbot of Dinas Basi (Basingwerk), he emphasized the liberality of the abbot's table: he had so many guests that two sittings were necessary, and he provided a choice of wines from Aragon, Brittany, and Spain.[6]

6

Cultural Achievements

The marriage between the Mediterranean culture introduced with Christianity and the native culture of the Celts produced an exciting cultural fusion in the Celtic churches. Some aspects of the introduced culture never took root in western Britain: the durable and grandiose stone architecture of Rome was alien to the British tradition of unsubstantial buildings, normally of timber or turf. But Christian literature and stone-carving and metalwork and so forth transplanted more readily into the Celtic world, and it was the Celtic church's patronage of these arts that has ensured that something of the spirit of the Celtic Church in Wales has survived throughout the centuries, and can be recaptured by us today from the pages of time-worn manuscripts, from the weathered surface of lichen-grown stone.

Latin was the official language of the Roman Empire: like English in the British Empire, it allowed communication between peoples of diverse tongues. The Church, proud of its Latin cultural heritage, retained Latin as its speech, and Latin helped to unify the Church, as it had done the Empire. Even after the Church in Wales had been isolated for many centuries from the continental Church, its more educated officials were familiar with Latin, so that when contact was renewed with other branches of the Church, communication was the least important problem. Asser was able to enter the service of King Alfred and be made a bishop of the English Church; the Normans were able to understand and borrow from the works of Welsh ecclesiastical scholars—Gildas, Nennius, and the rest. And of course, in days when translations were rarities, it was knowledge of Latin that made the Bible, the works of the Church Fathers, and other Christian literature available to the British Christians.

To judge from the number of Latin loan words found in

Welsh, Breton, and Cornish, the British language from which these three tongues evolved had been influenced by a period of widespread bilingualism in mainland Britain.[1] One would expect that during the Roman occupation Latin would have been most widely spoken in the Romanized south-east; then, when the Roman troops were withdrawn, the language would slowly have declined in use—though refugees from the barbarian advance may have reinforced the use of Latin in the highlands of north and west Britain. Meanwhile the Church was gathering strength, and it was the Church that was to take over education and keep Latin alive as a scholarly tongue in the succeeding centuries. In the fifth century, St Patrick wrote 'clumsy, but living and dynamic Latin'.[2] Clumsy, because it was for him very much a second language; living, because many colloquialisms slipped in from fifth-century spoken Latin of continental type, showing that Patrick had been in contact with Latin used as an everyday language. Indeed, in his *Confession* Patrick bears witness that some of his contemporaries had spoken Latin from their infancy, and some had undertaken extensive courses of study; he laments his own inferiority, his lack of these accomplishments. Gildas's Latin, on the other hand, is remarkably free of colloquialisms: it is very much the artificial language of the schoolroom. Clearly Gildas was one of those who had benefited from superior education, but he did not come from a Latin-speaking society. His style is close to that of the fifth-century Roman rhetoricians. He writes in complex Latin periods, using a wide and often strained vocabulary and bedecking his tirade with a range of references not only to the Bible, which was Patrick's sole source of inspiration, but to various of the Latin Church Fathers. However, whereas Patrick's writings, however lacking in polish, are appealingly direct, Gildas's pedantic verbal expertise can hardly be called attractive.

In the immediate post-Roman centuries, when Patrick and Gildas were writing, we find from genealogies and the names on early Christian stone monuments that some of the British princes and aristocracy of the highland zone were giving their children Latin names (though Celtic names are more common). This need be no more than an affectation, and the fashion soon fell from

101

favour. By the seventh century Latin-derived names had become extremely rare. Of course, the inscriptions themselves are mostly in Latin, for the memorials were a Roman fashion, taken over by the Latin-using Church. But one wonders how many people except for the clergy would have been able to understand the language in which they were written, let alone have been able to read it.

As the Roman occupation receded into the past, one would expect that Latin would have become all the more the preserve of a learned, Church-educated élite. We have too little evidence to trace the vicissitudes of Latin scholarship in Wales in pre-Norman times. By the ninth century, King Alfred was able to look towards the Welsh Church, to Asser, to help revitalize learning in England following the degeneration in scholarship resultant from the onslaught of the Vikings. Asser was a competent if verbose writer: his style, like that of some Anglo-Saxon writers such as Aldhelm, is sometimes reminiscent of the tortuously elaborate rhetorical style developed by Celtic scholars and known as Hisperic Latin after the most notorious example, the work known as the *Hisperica Famina*. Obscurity is the essence of this type of prose: its writers revel in rare words and difficult constructions. Latin has become a scholarly conceit, far removed from natural speech. Asser's *Life of Alfred* seems a cumbersome, pedantic work to those accustomed to more lucid prose. Somewhat earlier, Nennius, probably based in Gwynedd, had been writing more simply, but with little polish. From time to time Welsh idiom slipped into his Latin prose, showing not only his indebtedness to native sources, but his failure to re-think these sources in the Latin tongue.

Latin-based, literate culture arrived in a Britain where oral, native literature was highly developed and respected. Inevitably one would expect conflict, especially as much of the native legends and folklore would be moulded in pagan ways of thought, incompatible with the Christian way of interpreting the world. Gildas found the praise-poems with which the court bards celebrated the deeds of the princes especially obnoxious: to him, Maelgwn's bards were 'the rascally crew, yelling forth like Bacchanalian revellers'—it would be more fitting for Maelgwn to be listening to the praises of God. To some extent the new culture may well have been welcomed by the British aristocracy, who had already acquired some taste for Roman refinements. The early Christian stone monuments show that the people were finding in the new media ways to express their own values: the Christian memorial inscriptions employ Latin literacy to give expression to the age-old Celtic lust for glory. Like praise-poems, they immortalize the remembered person's name. In literature the same blend of the old and new values made an early appearance. In the earliest surviving British poem, the basically sixth-century *Gododdin*, a warrior, Rhufon the Tall, earns praise because 'he presented gold to the altar and gifts and fine presents to the minstrel'; donations to the Church have taken their place as part of the generosity proper to a Celtic hero. A purist such as Gildas could not stomach this sort of compromise, and there were always some who held to his views that secular literature was unworthy entertainment or reading for Christians. In the twelfth-century *Life of St Teilo*, Teilo and Maidoc are found reading, but the hagiographer is careful to stress that they are reading 'not the inventions of the poets, nor the ancient histories, but the Lamentations of the Prophet Jerome' (para. 8). However, just as many works by pagan classical authors survived condemnation by the early Church Fathers, so it was impossible in the Celtic lands for the Church to extinguish the vigorous bardic tradition; still less could it hope to eliminate from the minds of the people the folklore with which they were imbued.

Ultimately, both secular, Welsh literature and the Latin literature of the Church benefited from the cultural assimilation that took place. The native poets came to include Christian subjects in their repertoire. The Welsh Laws provide that the bard shall start his recital with a poem to God. In the *Black Book of Carmarthen* (one of a handful of medieval manuscripts that preserve collections of early Welsh literature) there are a number of poems on Christian themes—though they are often simple verses, probably intended for religious instruction. A more sophisticated verse is that in praise of St Padarn's staff, which was written in a space in a late-eleventh-century copy of St Augustine's *De Trinitate*. In a story in the *Life of St Gwynllyw* (para. 11), we hear of 'A certain

103

British versifier, versifying in British, [who] composed verses on his own race, and in the British speech praises concerning the manner of life of the most holy Gwynllyw and of his life's miracles . . .' Three-quarters of the way through a composition, the poet's inspiration fails him: but a serious flood threatens his life, and provides just the impetus he needs. Perched on a rooftop, he rapidly completes his poem, lest the waters should overwhelm him before he has finished.

The native language and literature eventually succeeded in carving out a niche for themselves in the world of church scholarship. Even in the comparatively early days of British Christianity, we find a non-Latin language embodied in writing: Irish, the language of the Ogam inscriptions. This is remarkable, for Britain is the only ex-Roman province where early Christian inscriptions appear in the native as well as in the Latin tongue.[3] The Ogam alphabet seems to have originated in southern Ireland, where Ogam inscriptions are most numerous. It was obviously intended to give a means of written expression to a people who did not use Latin—but presumably it was contact with Latin literacy (perhaps that introduced into Ireland by the earliest Christian missionaries) that sparked off the original idea. The alphabet is a simple sign-system, rather like morse code or semaphore: it consists of strokes, cut in groups above, below, or across a base-line. Thus one stroke crossing the line and at right-angles to it is equivalent to the letter *a*; two strokes to *o*; three to *u*; four to *e*; five to *i*. Similarly, five other letters are represented by groups of one to five strokes above the line, another five by strokes below the line, and a final five by slanting strokes across the line.[4] The system is so well suited to carving on wood that this would seem to have been the original medium, explaining the ease with which the alphabet was spread by Irish immigrants and travellers to western and south-western Britain. Most of the Ogam inscriptions in Wales seem to be of fifth- or sixth-century date, like the southern Irish examples. They are concentrated in the north-west and south-west of Wales, and in the Brecon area, where Irish settlement was heaviest. But they do not just show that the Irish in these areas were following the fashions of their homeland: unlike the Ogam stones in Ireland, many of those in Wales (indeed, all of those in the north-west) are bilingual, bearing a Latin inscription in the Roman alphabet as well as an Irish inscription in Ogam. Though the irregular use of a native tongue for memorial inscriptions might be tolerated, the Latin culture of the Church was making itself felt.

Ogam was in any case an importation: it was quite another matter for Welsh to find its way into script. But a unique memorial inscription from Towyn, Merioneth,[5] provides us with an early example of written Welsh. The inscription, carved clumsily on all four faces of a thin stone pillar, reads: '+ CINGEN CELEN ᛉ // TRICET / NITANAM // + TENGRUIN MALTE / [C?] GU/ADGAN//ANTERUNC DUBUT MARCIA'.[6] This may look incomprehensible to those familiar with modern Welsh: but beneath the archaic spelling lies a tongue basically similar to Welsh today. The words are mostly a string of names: 'The body of Cingen lies beneath. Egryn, Mallteg, Gwaddian, together with Dyfod and Marchiau.' If the seventh-to-ninth-century date ascribed by Nash-Williams is correct, we can see that, at the same time when the native language was influencing Nennius's prose, so it was battling against Latin's monopoly of memorial inscriptions. And this was a most significant move. From an early date, Celtic names had been transcribed in the Roman alphabet; now the Welsh language in general had been fitted into the alphabet devised to suit the Latin tongue. Ogam script could have but limited application—it was essentially a sign-language, for carved or incribed messages: the Ogam inscriptions normally give no more than the name of the deceased. The Roman alphabet was infinitely adaptable, for use on stone or parchment or wax tablets, for scratching in sand or scoring in wood. The marriage of the Welsh language with the Roman script opened the way for the oral literature of Wales to evolve slowly into a written literature— for there is a great distance between the two.

From the eighth century onwards we find odd scraps of Welsh written in manuscripts: the Latin texts take priority, but the church scribes sometimes saw fit to scribble in a Welsh verse or memorandum in a margin or blank space. There are Welsh records in the *Book of Lichfield*; Welsh verses written into a ninth-century copy of Juvencus (Cambridge University Library,

MS. Ff.4.42); the Welsh poem on St Padarn's staff written on folio 11ᵃ of Ieuan ap Sulien's copy of St Augustine's *De Trinitate* (Corpus Christi College, Cambridge, MS.199). But most of the scribes' time was spent on copies of the Gospels and Christian writings, not on recording a native literature that was not only essentially secular, but was adequately preserved in oral form. The scribes were working to the glory of God and his saints: Ieuan ap Sulien heads several pages of his copy of St Augustine's writings with invocations to God and various saints. When the *Black Book of Carmarthen* was written—probably in the twelfth century—religious poems were scattered throughout the otherwise non-religious contents as if to stress that God was still being kept in mind. Most of our copies of early Welsh literature date from well after the Norman conquest, by which time the oral tradition was weakening, and new cultural contacts were encouraging a fresh interest in reviving and perpetuating the old tales.

The native literature did have a strong influence upon some of the later writers within the Celtic Church in Wales. Not only does Nennius draw on native traditions and folklore for his historical compilation, but the *Lives* of the Welsh Saints, especially Lifris's late-eleventh-century *Life of St Cadog*, are superb examples of the way in which popular legends could be drawn into a Christian context.

———

In the Roman Empire, grammar schools existed to train potential administrators and lawyers in literacy and other basic skills. As these schools deteriorated or closed down with the Empire's decline, the needs of the Church for an educated, literate clergy led to the development of specifically Christian schools. These might be under the patronage of a bishop, or run by a local priest; as monasticism spread, monasteries became important centres of education. In Britain, especially in the highland areas, the city life which would have made it possible for boys to attend school daily in the house of a bishop was lacking: monastic schools were the most convenient.

The monasteries functioned like boarding-schools. There children would be cared for, taught, and disciplined in return for an appropriate endowment or fee. The system would have been easily acceptable to the Celtic aristocracy, who were already accustomed to send their children to 'foster-parents' for upbringing. Some of the pupils at the monastic schools would be dedicated by their parents to a life in the Church; others would be free to choose whether or not to return to secular life. The normal age for education to begin in the Roman world was seven. It was at this age that the *Life of St Cybi* says he began to learn his letters (para. 2), and that Cadog according to his *Life* was sent to be taught by the hermit Meuthi (para. 1). For the most able and resourceful, education might continue well into adult life; and when local facilities had been exhausted there was always the possibility of continuing one's studies overseas. The education with which St Cadog is credited is exhaustive: after twelve years of instruction from Meuthi 'in sacred literature and liberal training' (*Life of St Cadog*, para. 6), he founded his first monastery, but soon set off for Ireland, where he studied at Lismore for three years, gaining 'perfection in all western knowledge' (para. 10). On his return, he sought out yet another teacher, the 'celebrated rhetorician' Bachan, who had recently arrived from Italy, for Cadog greatly desired 'to be instructed by him in Latinity after the Roman manner' (para. 11). In his reference to Bachan's teaching, the hagiographer is influenced by the new educational opportunities opened up in his own time by contact through the Normans with Rome. In Cadog's day, it would have been the Irish who offered the summit of education: the Irish quickly became distinguished if idiosyncratic Christian scholars, and judging both from the literature they have left us, and from their reputation in their own time, soon surpassed most of their British colleagues in scholarly skill.

There were a few textbooks—such as the Latin grammars, 'Donatus and Priscian', by which St Cadog is said to have been taught (*Life of St Cadog*, para. 6)—but on the whole the teacher had very little in the way of teaching-aids except his own knowledge, and his skill in sharing it. It is individual teachers, rather than centres of learning, that are celebrated in Welsh tradition: Paulinus, who was reputedly St David's teacher, and, most famous of all, St Illtud (perhaps identical with the unnamed, distinguished teacher with whom Gildas says King Maelgwn studied for a time).

Lengthy professional training was already required in secular society for artists and craftsmen: bards, story-tellers, blacksmiths, and so forth. The ecclesiastical students, like their lay counterparts, seem to have entered on a sort of scholastic apprenticeship: advanced students would pursue their own studies, like St David's disciple, Aidan, who in a passage in the *Life of St David* is found sitting 'out of doors, reading to confirm the meaning of a doctrine' (para. 35). What these students would value would be the chance to consult their master on special problems, and the use of his library—though even the best library would have been strictly limited in its range of manuscripts. Only a few works, notably the Gospels and other works of Scripture, were widely known: the Bible was the basis of Celtic Christian belief and practice. Extending the range of a library meant procuring copies of additional works, or borrowing them so that copies could be made: both methods were costly in their own way. The best way of broadening one's reading was to travel from library to library in search of new books. Thus, from a widely read teacher a pupil could gain knowledge that it would otherwise take him years to acquire.

To us, used as we are to an educational system geared to instil the maximum amount of information in the minimum of time, the education provided within the early Welsh Church seems very limited. The student did not have tens and hundreds of books to master: he could not have mastered them in such numbers, for he was reading script, not neat print, and punctuation and spelling were far less standardized and easy to follow than today. Moreover, the words, especially of Scripture, were not regarded simply as symbols contributing towards an overall meaning, but as each of great significance in itself, to be pondered over and interpreted in minute detail. St David's wisdom was represented by Rhigyfarch as his ability '[to perceive] the spiritual meaning within a literal statement' (*Life of St David*, para. 2). Several manuscripts survive from the time of the Celtic Church, which have been glossed in Welsh: that is, beside the

Latin words, notes on the meaning and interpretation have been added in Welsh. Sometimes Irish as well as Welsh glosses occur in the same manuscript, showing that Irish and Welsh scholars were working side by side. For instance, a manuscript of Juvencus, now in Cambridge (University Library MS. Ff.4.42), was copied by an Irish scribe, Nuada, probably in the ninth century, and Nuada seems to have been working at a Welsh *scriptorium*, for he himself glossed the work both in Irish and in Welsh. Further glosses in both languages were added at a later date.

One aspect of the Celtic scholars' approach to Scriptural interpretation was their concern with numerical symbolism. Geometry and arithmetic were important not solely for their practical value in explaining and controlling the natural world, but for their spiritual significance. Since God had created nature, the laws of nature, including number, embodied divine truths. The saints' *Lives* are heavily influenced by the tradition of numerical symbolism: an excellent example is the description of St Cadog's baptism in the *Life of St Cadog* (para. 1). The infant Cadog is said to have reached the well, where he was to be baptized, by three unaided leaps: 'the three leaps', it is explained, '. . . denote the mystic number of the Holy Trinity, that is, the Father and the Son and the Holy Ghost, whose service he continually with all his might brought to effect.' Undoubtedly the Celtic love of such allusions sprang from deeper roots than Christianity in Britain could boast: Celtic mythology and secular literature are similarly imbued with number's mystical significance. The same wondrous number, three, that underlies the Trinity is the basis of a distinctive Celtic literary device, the Triad, which groups in threes things with some factor in common.[7]

Apart from learning to read and write in Latin, and studying the Bible, potential clerics would need to learn the psalms, canticles, hymns, and basic rites of the Church. Rhigyfarch relates how St David 'was taught his letters, and learned the Church practices' (*Life of St David*, para. 8) before being ordained as a priest: it was only then that he went to Paulinus to pursue more advanced studies. No early British liturgical book has survived. Presumably the British liturgy was closely related to its Irish cousin—indeed, according to Irish tradition David, Gilla, and Doco (David, Gildas, and Cadog) introduced a new form of the Mass to Ireland. However, the Irish liturgy too is imperfectly known; it was replaced in the eleventh century by the Roman liturgy, into which just a few Irish-derived customs, such as the chanting of the Creed at Mass, seem to have found their way.[8]

In the Western Church as a whole, celebration of the saints came to play an increasingly important part in church services, especially from the eighth century on. Saints were invoked in the liturgy, and martyrologies (lists of saints with the dates of their festivals) were drawn up to give the clergy guidance as to which saints merited commemoration. By about A.D. 800 the Irish were adapting imported martyrologies by entering their own saints: the Welsh Saint David was among the names included in the Martyrology of Tallaght at this time—which is probably the earliest known evidence for David's cult.

From Wales we have a late-eleventh-century martyrology, found with a copy of the Psalter copied for Rhigyfarch by a scribe, Ithael (Trinity College, Dublin, MS. A.4.20). Here too local saints are added to an imported martyrology: but David is not among them. St Padarn is included, however, showing that when this manuscript was written Rhigyfarch's interest lay in his home at Llanbadarn Fawr, not in St David's, whose patron's *Life* he was later to write.

By the twelfth century, saints' *Lives* had become a popular source of readings at divine services—which is scarcely surprising, when one considers their entertainment value and conformity to native literary taste, as well as their edifying content. Here was a world the audience could understand: a world of heroes and villains, good and evil, where (as with the cartoon-stories of today) everything was undemanding, clear-cut, larger than life. It is surely no coincidence that now the production of saints' *Lives* suddenly flourished in Wales: some of these *Lives* were patently intended for reading aloud on the saints' festivals. The first version of *St Carannog's Life* begins: 'This festival is to be solemnized by all people believing in God . . .', while the *Life of St Padarn* concludes with an invitation to the congregation: 'Let us, therefore, pray most holy Padarn that . . . we through his intercession may dwell in the heavenly realms' (para. 29). The longer *Lives* may have been intended for private reading by scholars, or for reading aloud in instalments to the clergy, perhaps at meal-times: the *Life of St Teilo* opens with an address to the 'most loved brethren', while the *Life of St Cadog* draws a point to the attention of 'all reading and hearing the Life of the pious father' (para. 9). These longer *Lives* would be a fruitful source for clerics in search of raw material for sermons on the saints' virtues—perhaps, to reach a wider section of the public, preached in Welsh.

In their original Latin form, the *Lives* would have reached only a limited, educated audience. But the arrival of educated men among the Norman settlers increased the audience for such works. As we have seen, many of the *Lives* incorporate propaganda designed to deter attacks on churches and interference with their customary rights, and, especially in the case of the *Lives* written in the interests of Llandaff, to gain Norman support in internal disputes within the Church in Wales. The strong Breton element in several of the *Lives* can be explained by the arrival with the Normans of Breton settlers: Canon G. H. Doble has suggested that the settlement in Monmouth of the Baderon family from near Dol may account for the frequent references to the saints of Dol in the *Lives* of the Welsh saints.

It is unrealistic to judge the *Lives* by modern standards of history and biography. The authors of the *Lives* seem to have had little information at all relevant to the saints to help them. Even the old charters re-used by the authors of the *Life of St Cadog* and the *Book of Llandaff*, and the early monastic rule Rhigyfarch seems to have discovered, were rare survivals: as Rhigyfarch himself tells us, those old manuscripts that had survived were 'eaten away along the edges and backs by the continuous gnawing of worms and the ravages of passing years' (*Life of St David*, ch. 66). Moreover, since the *Lives* were didactic in intent, historical accuracy was not of great importance: they had succeeded in their purpose if they managed to impress their audience with the saints' virtues and powers. If the *Lives* look like gullible and unscrupulous fabrications, the same could be said of the stories about Arthur—who, like the saints, seems to have been a real person who attracted all sorts of legends after the true facts about him had been forgotten: yet we still find the tales about Arthur compellingly attractive. As Caerwyn Williams has pointed out in an essay full of insight on the *Bucheddau* (the medieval Welsh versions of the *Lives* of the saints),[9] the *Lives* are in fact best seen as religious romances: 'the same world that produced the tales of Arthur . . . produced the tales of the saints'. They were both designed to appeal to the native audience, and borrowed from native traditions so that they could exercise that appeal. When they go into minute and improbable detail, this, as Caerwyn Williams explains, was an appropriate response to the audience's level of understanding: like children, the uneducated public would have found little to interest them in tales unrelated to their own experience. They wanted to be told, not just that St Cadog used to go into retreat at Lent, but *where* he went (*Life of St Cadog*, para. 18); not just that there was a holy well dedicated to St Gwynllyw, but *why* and *when* and *how* it had come into being (*Life of St Gwynllyw*, para. 9). Names and incidents from secular literature were drawn in to enliven the *Lives*, especially by Lifris, author of the vivid original version of the *Life of St Cadog*. For instance, Cadog, when founding a monastery in Scotland, is said to have unearthed the collar-bone 'of some ancient hero, monstrous and enormous . . . through which . . . a champion on horseback could . . . ride without check' (para. 26). Miraculously, the owner of the collar-bone is brought back to life: it is the giant Caw Prydein. We cannot reconstruct Caw's role in secular legend in detail, but nineteen sons of Caw are among Arthur's court in the early Arthurian tale of *Culhwch ac Olwen* (in the *Mabinogion*), while one son, Gwarthegyt, figures in another *Mabinogion* story, the *Dream of Rhonabwy*. The Church claimed that Gildas was a son of Caw—though this tradition occurs no earlier than the *Life of St Cadog*, and the twelfth-century Breton *Life of St Gildas of Rhuys*.

Since the founders' kin sometimes retained rights over the succession to religious foundations, one would expect that at least the descent of the saints would have been remembered. But it seems that, by the time the saints' *Lives* came to be written, this information had been lost. When detailed genealogies of the saints are provided in the *Lives*, these are additions to the basic texts—like the genealogy of St David, found only in the late Vespasian version of his *Life*, and that of St Cadog (paras. 45–7), identified by Dr Emmanuel as an addition.[10] It is not until the thirteenth century that we find the earliest manuscript copies of saintly genealogies: maybe it was actually the production of the Saints' *Lives* that stimulated speculation as to the saints' origins.

To function effectively, the Church needed to keep various records. The calendars used to record saints' days and other Christian festivals were only one example. Computational tables were needed for calculating the date on which Easter would fall each year; and it may have been from notes jotted in the margins of these tables that the custom of keeping annals (year-by-year records of events) evolved in Britain. As yet, the system of counting years from the birth of Christ had not become fashionable (it was the eighth-century English writer, Bede, who pioneered the use of this system in historical writing). The cycles of years recorded in the Easter tables would have provided a convenient framework for chronological records of events. But this remains a hypothesis. No genuine annals survive from the early centuries of the life of the Celtic Church in the area that is now Wales.[11] From the late eighth century on, annals were kept at St David's, and before long, entries for earlier centuries, extracted mainly from Irish annals and from a North British chronicle, were prefaced to these annals. A copy was made of the whole collection in the mid-tenth century, and from this copy the annals found their way, in the company of the *Historia Brittonum*, into a manuscript executed by an Anglo-Norman scribe at some unidentified scriptorium in *c*.A.D. 1100 (British Museum Harleian MS. 3859).[12] Meanwhile annals continued to be kept at St David's, right up to and beyond the arrival of the Normans. Interestingly, by the 1160s the interest of the annalists has shifted towards English affairs, reflecting the increasing Anglicization of the see. The monks of the Cistercian monasteries which the Normans founded in Wales, especially of Strata Florida, also proved active chroniclers, and their Latin annals were to provide the basis of the famous Welsh chronicles, the *Bruts*.[13]

To tell the time of day when church services should be held, sundials (or 'mass-clocks') were used both in Ireland and in Anglo-Saxon England; and a surviving example at Clynnog Fawr shows that they were also in use in Wales. The Clynnog Fawr sundial is thought to be of eleventh- or early-twelfth-century date. Today it stands in the churchyard to the south-west of St Beuno's Chapel; it is a tall, pale slab of stone, with an incised semicircle at the top of the main face. At the nucleus of the semicircle is a little hole, in which a style to cast a shadow would have been inserted. Lines divide the semicircle into four segments; by the octaval system, used both in England and in Ireland, the twenty-four-hour day was divided into eight equal 'tides'.

Although some Latin works by scholars writing in Wales have survived, we can seldom discover much about the writers' backgrounds and the context within which they worked. The *Historia Brittonum* attributed to Nennius makes reference in chronological calculations to the fourth year of King Merfyn's reign, and it seems likely that this mish-mash of historical materials was compiled under the patronage of that eminent mid-ninth-century king of Gwynedd. Merfyn traced his descent from a North British dynasty, which would explain the northern bias of much of Nennius's material; and Merfyn took a lively interest in scholarship, as a strange little anecdote reveals. We learn from a letter that was forwarded to an Irish teacher, Colgu, that Merfyn liked to pose a test to those Irish scholars who stayed at his court (probably on their way to the Continent). The puzzle had in fact been devised by an Irishman: it was a cryptogram, in which the message 'Mermin [i.e. Merfyn] the King greets Concenn' [14] could be revealed by substituting Greek for Latin letters. Dubthach, the inventor of the puzzle, had believed that 'no Irish scholar, far less a British one' would be able to solve it; but the group of Irish scholars who wrote the letter to Colgu had managed to solve it, and quickly sent the solution to Colgu so that later travellers could be forewarned! One implication of this story is that contemporary Irish scholarship was superior to that in Wales, since Dubthach considered the British even less likely than the Irish to solve his puzzle; and certainly Nennius's fascinating but clumsily written work would bear this out. Nennius himself seems to have shared Merfyn's playful approach to scholarship, for he was said to have invented an alphabet on the spur of the moment to refute the jibe of a Saxon scholar that the British had no alphabet of their own.[15]

On the eve of the Norman subjugation of the Celtic Church in Wales, we find evidence that a distinguished family of scholars was at work in south-west Wales. This was the family of Sulien, Bishop of St David's, who were influential both at their native Llanbadarn Fawr and at St David's for several generations.[16] Sulien himself, we learn from a poem by one of his sons, Ieuan, was of noble birth, and his education had included instruction in Scotland and Ireland. When he was made Bishop of St David's in 1073 he was already over sixty years old, and five years later he retired; but he was recalled after Norse raiders had slain his successor. This tough old man cannot have lacked courage: not until 1085 did he again retire, and then he lived on for another six years. All was instability in his time: apart from the Norse, there were the first westward thrusts of the Normans, and internal rivalries between the Welsh princes. William the Conqueror visited St David's during Sulien's episcopate; and when the exiled King of Gwynedd, Gruffydd ap Cynan, landed at Porth Clais and allied himself with Rhys ap Tewdwr of Ceredigion, Sulien blessed the alliance of these rulers, who were to establish themselves as the most powerful kings in Wales.

It is hard to believe that Sulien can have had much time for scholarly pursuits during his episcopate. But previously the school of Llanbadarn Fawr had been under his direction; according to the *Brut*, Rhigyfarch was educated solely by Sulien, and presumably this applied also to Sulien's other sons. Rhigyfarch's most famous work is his *Life of St David*. This celebration of the founder of the church where his father was bishop is a controlled and scholarly work, following the best hagiographical tradition by proceeding in orderly fashion from the first signs that foretell the unborn saint's distinction to the miracles that follow his death. Rhigyfarch claims that he has gathered material about the saint 'for an example to us all, and the Father's glory' (ch. 66). He is at pains to stress David's pre-eminence among the Welsh saints, but the *Life* is relatively free of the precise definitions of the property

115

and rights of the saint's foundations that give most other *Lives* of the Welsh saints so defensive an air. Also written by Rhigyfarch, but very different in atmosphere, is a Latin poem which, with its description of the miseries besetting the Welshmen of south-west Wales following the Welsh rebellion against the Normans in 1093, gives us an insight into the unsettled conditions under which Sulien's family were working.[17]

Ieuan, one of Rhigyfarch's brothers, is probably the arch-presbyter of Llanbadarn, 'wisest of the wise', whose death the *Brut* records in 1137. He illuminated a copy of the Psalter (Trinity College, Dublin, MS.A.4.20) which was written for Rhigyfarch by a scribe, Ithael; and he wrote a copy of St Augustine's *De Trinitate* (Corpus Christi College, Cambridge, MS.199), adding on the fly-leaf his own poem about his father, at whose request the copy was made. A third brother, Daniel, became archdeacon of Powys, and was the Welsh candidate for the bishopric of St David's in 1115—a post he lost to the Norman candidate, Bernard. Daniel's son, Cydifor, became Archdeacon of Cardigan, while Rhigyfarch's son, a second Sulien, was brought up by the clergy at Llanbadarn and became a lawyer. A third grandson of Sulien, Henry (son of an otherwise-unknown Arthen), is said by the *Brut* to have been the leading scholar in Wales, though nothing of his work has survived. With this third generation, Sulien's family disappears from record. They were remarkable not only for their scholarship, but for their ability to procure and retain high ecclesiastical office after the Norman infiltration of the Welsh Church had meant that men of Norman blood were preferred for high church appointments in Wales.

In Glamorgan, there seems to have been another distinguished family of scholars at this date, though less is known of them.[18] Lifris, author of the *Life of St Cadog*, was the son of Herwald, the late-eleventh-century Bishop of Glamorgan; the family was apparently based at Cadog's chief foundation, Llancarfan. Lifris has a far less sober approach to hagiography than his contemporary, Rhigyfarch. He delights in the exuberance of the native folklore he weaves into his narrative: revenge is swift and merciless, miracles often bizarre. The *Life* has all the colour and savagery that gives bite to the *Mabinogion* and the Irish sagas. A murdered man, beheaded by his slayers, rises from the dead 'bearing his head in his bosom, and carrying a great stone on his back, wet and bloody, of maimed and horrid aspect' (para. 21); cows paid to King Arthur in compensation for a crime are first of all miraculously turned into the colour he has demanded—'distinguished in their fore part with a red colour and in their hind part with white'—and then, because of the fickleness of his demand, are turned into worthless bundles of fern (para. 22). This is entertainment rather than didacticism. Yet, as we have seen, the *Life* did have a very real practical purpose: Llancarfan was handed over to St Peter's, Gloucester, in the early stages of the Norman advance into Wales; and the detailed definitions of the lands owned by Cadog and of the rights he procured for Llancarfan, given both in Lifris's *Life* and in later additions to it, present the case against this seizure.

Eventually, the family of scholars from Llancarfan turned their attention towards building up the see of Llandaff, where Urban (another relative of Herwald, and his successor as bishop) founded his cathedral in the early twelfth century. The experience gained by the family of Llancarfan in compiling St Cadog's *Life* proved invaluable when they entered on their most ambitious undertaking, the *Book of Llandaff*. This twelfth-century manuscript is an astute compilation of materials in support of Llandaff's claims to a long and orthodox past and an extensive diocese, and it includes the *Lives* of the three alleged founders of Llandaff, with charters attributed to the lifetime of each saint and to the lifetimes of subsequent bishops of the see.

A note identifies the author of the *Life of St Teilo* in the *Book of Llandaff* as Lifris's brother, Stephen; Lifris seems to have taken no part in the work—presumably he was dead. By now his *Life of St Cadog* was out of date, and it was rewritten to suit the new interests of the Llancarfan family by Caradoc of Llancarfan. Caradoc seems to have made hagiography his speciality: he is known to have written other *Lives*, including a *Life of St Gildas* written in the interests of Glastonbury. Most of the *Lives* of the south-eastern Welsh saints, written after Lifris had set the fashion with his *Life of St Cadog*, are similar in content and style to Caradoc's work: it seems that he was just one of a school of hagiographers writing against the background of the consolidation of Llandaff's position.

With Caradoc and his colleagues we have left the world of the Celtic Church behind. Caradoc toned down Lifris's *Life of St Cadog*, suppressing the more violent and unchristian passages: for instance, he saw fit to save Cadog's disciples, Barruc and Walees, from the fate which befell them in Lifris's version, where they were drowned for no more heinous crime than forgetting a book (para. 29). Caradoc was influenced by the more refined literary taste introduced by the Normans: he was a contemporary of Geoffrey of Monmouth, whose famous *History of the Kings of Britain* transformed the warrior-hero Arthur of native tradition into the courtly figure of Arthurian romance. It was men such as these, Norman in sympathy and often at least part-Norman in blood, who were to take the lead in scholarship in the Church in Wales from now on.

We possess very few manuscripts copied by the scribes of the Celtic Church in Wales. Those that survived the Viking raids had later hazards to face: for instance, in 1550, the protestant Bishop Farrar ordered all the sacred books at St David's to be destroyed. The Celts developed their own distinctive style of script and manuscript decoration, but these are best known from Irish or Hiberno-Saxon[19] examples. In Wales, the development of the Celtic half-uncial script can be traced better in the inscriptions on stone monuments than in manuscripts. The fifth- and most of the sixth-century inscriptions are in classical Roman lettering, little different from that used on monuments in Romano-British times. But gradually more and more rounded letter-forms work their way into the inscriptions, borrowed from the Roman half-uncial script which had become popular in Italy and southern Gaul by about A.D. 600. This rounded script was in part derived from the cursive, or flowing, writing used for manuscripts in the Eastern Mediterranean lands, showing yet again the influence of the Eastern Empire upon the early Celtic churches and their culture. The Celtic scribes developed a distinctive script of their own from the imported half-uncial lettering, and this is the script still used for printing Irish today. By the seventh century the script was established: in Wales, one of the earliest examples is the grandiose inscription to King Cadfan of Gwynedd at Llangadwaladr, Anglesey.[20] This inscription contains a few Roman capitals, but half-uncials predominate.

We know that some of the Welsh churches possessed venerated copies of the Gospels. From the British Isles as a whole just a very few sumptuous copies of the Gospels in Irish or Hiberno-Saxon style have survived—most famous being the glorious eighth- or early-ninth-century *Book of Kells*, perhaps produced by Irish monks on Iona. The only one of these books which could possibly have been produced in Wales is the *Book of Lichfield*, or Gospels of St Chad (now in Lichfield Cathedral Library), which belonged to a church of St Teilo (probably Llandeilo Fawr) in the eighth or early ninth century. But just as the book later passed to Lichfield, so St Teilo's church may have obtained it from elsewhere. The foreign influences on the manuscript's decoration show that it was produced at a centre where Mediterranean art (in manuscripts, paintings, textiles, etc.) was known: this seems unlikely in Wales, where the acceptance of the Roman Easter date which opened up the way for contact with the continental Church was delayed until the later eighth century. Moreover, the contemporary carved stone crosses in Wales are generally inferior to Irish examples—is it likely that manuscript production was so much more advanced? On the other hand, the *Book of Lichfield* could have been the work of artists of the Hiberno-Saxon school working at a Welsh foundation: it has some similarities to the *Book of Lindisfarne*, another splendid Gospel book, executed by an Irish-trained Northumbrian who was Bishop of Lindisfarne.

Appreciation of the *Book of Lichfield* is hampered by the manuscript's damaged state: many pages are missing, the remainder are badly preserved, and the pigments have not just faded, but decomposed.[21] Originally the book would have been breathtaking. It was produced on the grand scale reserved for specially treasured Gospel books: with large pages (now clumsily trimmed), a beautiful capital script, and elaborate decoration including whole pages devoted to symbolic designs. Originally the opening page of each Gospel would have been faced by a stylized portrait of the Evangelist, though only the portraits of St Mark and St Luke survive. The decoration not only uses to the full the range of designs commonly used in Hiberno-Saxon manuscripts, but incorporates some new elements. Thus, to the animals that twist and weave their way through the patterns of Hiberno-Saxon art are added new types of beast and long-necked birds borrowed from Mediterranean art of the sixth and seventh centuries; while the Celtic spirals and fretwork are varied by use of an Eastern motif, the key-pattern. The result is a riotous exuberance of pattern and (originally) colour: to quote F. Henry, 'everything is set in motion . . . The letters suddenly turn into monsters, which, with wild, protruding eyes, bite their own necks. The frames unexpectedly curl up into a pair of legs or develop a biting snout . . . [There are] constant surges of invention.'[22]

As we have seen, several manuscripts produced by the family of Sulien have survived: but these are manuscripts of a different class, intended for more mundane use than the prestigious Gospel books. The decoration is confined mainly to fine initial letters, and the range of colours is far more limited. In the *Book of Lichfield*, the original colours seem to have been purple, red, yellow, white, and various blues: Ieuan's copy of St Augustine's *De Trinitate* uses only green, black, and yellow; the Psalter copied for Rhigyfarch uses red, yellow, and green. But the manuscripts are skilfully written, and what decoration there is is finely executed.

The most durable remains of the craftsmanship practised within the Celtic Church in Wales have proved to be the Christian stone monuments, which in different forms were produced throughout the life of the Celtic Church. The earliest monuments, dating from the fifth and sixth centuries, are simple memorial stones, with a brief inscription in Latin or Ogam (or both), usually providing no more than the name of the deceased. Akin to these monuments is an isolated example of a leaden coffin, from Llangeinwen, Anglesey,[23] of fifth-century date, and inscribed with the name of the dead man, and perhaps with sacred monograms. As we have seen, the custom of erecting tombstones seems to have been re-imported into western Britain in a Christian context in post-Roman times, and some of the monuments may even have been the work of itinerant foreign craftsmen. But British culture soon made itself felt in the style of the monuments: before long inscriptions are found that read vertically, not horizontally, obviously as a result of influence from the vertical arrangement of the Ogam script. Sometimes the father or grandfather of the dead person is named, a sign of worldly concern that Christians elsewhere were careful to shun. As time went by, the orderly lettering of classical Roman inscriptions gave way to a rather confused mixture of styles, with the rounded, half-uncial script gradually rising to prominence. Sometimes letters were carved back-to-front or upside-down; and the Latin grammar of the inscriptions is often defective. These are not just signs of degeneracy: Celtic Christian culture was moving away from the borrowed culture of the classical Roman world towards a distinctive identity of its own.

Although the custom of carving commemorative inscriptions was imported from the Roman world, stone monuments had been erected in Wales since prehistoric times. The old standing stones made prominent landmarks before the landscape became littered with the telegraph poles and pylons and all the other paraphernalia of modern civilization: they attracted all sorts of tales and superstitions. In Brittany there are several examples of crosses added by Christians to prehistoric monuments, perhaps (as a story in the *Life of St Samson* (ch. 48) suggests) deliberately to counteract pagan rites formerly focused on them. A story in the *Life of St Cadog* purports to tell the origin of a standing stone, by means of which 'the Lord heals those who are unable to hold urine, and divers kinds of other diseases' (para. 21); possibly this was a prehistoric monument whose special powers had been Christianized. The early Christian stone monuments in Wales were not uninfluenced by the long tradition to which they were heirs. A unique Christian monument from Trecastle, Breconshire,[24] began life as a conventional memorial stone inscribed in Latin and Ogam; but at some later date it was re-used, and what had been the back of the stone was decorated with panels of incised symbols which, though dating from Christian times, are very similar to the prehistoric art found on megalithic and later monuments. The roughly shaped stones on which the Christian inscriptions were carved conformed to the philosophy of the pagan craftsmen: unlike the Romans, who, god-like, shaped their materials into regular, pre-determined forms, the Celtic craftsmen were more like catalysts, accentuating, not eliminating, the natural qualities of their stones.[25]

Nearer to our conception of art are the later Christian monuments, the stones inscribed with crosses and, most impressive of all, the free-standing sculpted crosses that marked the summit of the ecclesiastical stone-carvers' achievement. Occasionally incised symbols, including the cross and the sacred monogram, the Chi-Rho, are found on the early inscribed stones. From the seventh century onwards, the cross became the main feature of the stone monuments, and was only occasionally accompanied by inscriptions. The symbol of the cross owed its popularity to the fourth-century Roman Emperor, Constantine. Before he abolished crucifixion as a means of execution, the cross was too terrible an instrument to attract veneration. The British craftsmen adopted the cross in a variety of forms. There was the simple linear cross, formed by two intersecting lines, and the outline cross, which appeared as if the craftsman had traced around the edge of a substantial cross. There were also forms of the cross derived from the Chi-Rho, the monogram of Christ: those favoured in western Britain were the 'monogrammatic cross' (an equal-armed cross with a loop to the right side of the upper arm), and the ring-cross (an equal-armed cross enclosed in a ring). Looking from monument to monument in Wales, we can see the inventiveness with which these basic symbols were elaborated: the arms of the cross end in knobs, or fork like snakes' tongues; crosses are given double, or even treble outlines.

The cross-inscribed stones tend to be grouped around Christian establishments, such as Llanddewi Brefi, Nevern, and St Dogmael's, suggesting that these foundations patronized the craftsmen who produced the monuments. But it seems unlikely that the demand for stone-carving would have been sufficient to justify full-time and permanent employment of craftsmen; only about 150 cross-inscribed stones survive in Wales from the three centuries (c.A.D. 600–900) when they were in fashion. However, when, from the ninth century onwards, elaborate free-standing crosses came to be carved, the evidence is strongly suggestive that a few important churches supported schools of stone-carving. These late stone crosses are not only clustered around a relatively small number of major foundations, nearly all in South Wales (e.g. St David's, Penmon, and several churches in Glamorgan), but they show distinctive local styles. For instance, one type of cross, a slab carved on one or both faces with a partly sunken Maltese cross, is found only in the Margam, Merthyr Mawr, and Neath area of Glamorgan.[26]

It must be admitted that the Welsh crosses cannot compare with the finest examples of Irish and Northumbrian stone-carving. In Ireland, achievements in stone sculpture culminated in the production of magnificent Scripture crosses, elaborate free-standing crosses, embroidered all over with carvings, including Biblical scenes. Stone-carving was the aspect of church culture that was best able to survive the plundering and burning of the Viking raids, and it benefited from the new sources of inspiration provided by Viking craftsmanship. In Wales, perhaps the dual pressure from the Vikings on the one hand and the Anglo-Saxons on the other left too little energy and too few resources free to concentrate on the development of stone-carving: there are a few very fine crosses, but no sustained excellence. Indeed, it may be that foreign craftsmen—for intance, Irishmen fleeing from Viking attack—were responsible for some of the Welsh crosses, for these ambitious sculptures appear on the scene with suspicious suddenness in the ninth century, suggesting that this form of sculpture was introduced into the country, rather than being a native development.

The cross-decorated stones and the stone crosses had a wider range of functions than the fifth- and sixth-century memorial stones. The symbol of the cross could be understood by all, not just by the literate: it was a shorthand way of invoking a sense of awe at God's presence and power. As a token of Christ's triumph over death, the very image of the cross could set all evil to flight.

It was a Christian talisman, at once protective and awesome. Stones marked with crosses proved ideal for marking the boundaries of church lands, or places of special sanctity. In an Irish manuscript, the *Book of Mulling*, a plan of a monastery survives which shows that twelve crosses were placed within and around the monastic enclosure, several of them dedicated to evangelists and prophets: presumably the crosses were intended to protect the monastery and its precincts. A stone cross from Margam, Glamorgan,[27] inscribed '(The cross) of Peter. Ilquici . . . set up this cross', perhaps fulfilled a similar role. The *Life of St Dubricius* alleges that a stone was set up to mark the birth-place of the saint (para. 1): this is late evidence for the custom of erecting monuments to mark places where significant events had occurred, but the practice was of early origin in the Celtic lands, as we learn from the seventh-century *Life of St Columba*, which refers to two crosses erected on Iona, one to mark the spot where a man miraculously dropped dead, the other to mark the saint's place of residence at the time of his death.

As landmarks, stone monuments made convenient meeting-places. A charter appended to the *Life of St Cadog* records that the grant was confirmed 'near the cross, which is on the road known to many' (para. 63). Crosses were especially important as preaching-stations, to mark the spots where open-air services would be held. Often wooden crosses may have served this purpose (in England, a large wooden cross buried beneath the church of St Bertolin at Stafford was perhaps the preaching-cross used on the site before the church was built). Several of the Welsh crosses show influence from wooden or metal prototypes: the crosses inscribed on a group of stones from Anglesey have spiked feet, presumably in imitation of portable crosses; while the Glamorgan crosses in particular often have heavily moulded angles and bosses which would be more at home on crosses of metal or wood, where they would be needed to cover rivets or joints.

In Wales, some stone crosses were used, like the earlier inscribed stones, for commemorative purposes. This is in contrast to the practice in Ireland, where some specialization of functions had developed, with flat slabs being used as memorial-stones, while the free-standing crosses fulfilled other functions. Two types of cross had also emerged in Wales—the free-standing sculpted cross, and the stone slab with a cross worked in relief—but the latter was simply a stylistic variation, confined to south Wales.

Often the Welsh crosses are carved with the intricate designs—fretwork and spirals and knots—so beloved of the Celtic artists. Yet one may wonder what relevance these abstract patterns had to the monuments' Christian purpose. For though these designs were modified by exposure to art from other lands (often through Christian channels), ultimately they were rooted in the art of the pagan Celts. Paradoxically, it was the fact that they were pagan symbols that gave the patterns Christian relevance. With their teasing, maze-like quality, they are non-verbal riddles, symbolic of the mystical aspects of life, aspects in which the Christians were as interested as their pagan predecessors. These symbols could acquire new Christian meanings: for intance, the triskele (three linked loops) was used to represent the Trinity.[28]

When, rarely, the Welsh stone-carvers included human figures in their decorative scheme, these too were symbolic rather than representational. The viewer needed only a few clues to recognize that a human was depicted: the artist did not attempt an accurate imitation of reality. Rather, he treated the human figure in the same stylized way that he treated other elements in his decorative repertoire. The symbols that stand for men in Celtic art are squat, dumpy little figures, often with feet and arms sticking out at odd angles from the geometrical shapes which represent their clothes. Their stiffness may owe something to the limitations imposed on the artists when working in metal or wood. Three stone fragments from Glamorgan, of ninth- or tenth-century date, illustrate the style. The first, at Pontardawe,[29] is carved with a figure reminiscent of a man wearing sandwich-boards: beneath the decorated rectangular panel that stands for his tunic, his feet are splayed outwards like a ballet-dancer's. His arms are raised above his head in prayer. Another praying figure is represented on a stone fragment from Seven Sisters.[30] He wears a pleated skirt resembling a kilt secured by a belt around his waist. The third example, at Llanrhidian, Gower,[31] shows just how far the human figure could be assimilated to the geometrical shapes that are the building-blocks of Celtic art. Two humans are depicted on the stone: their faces are pear-shaped, their bodies are represented by patterned panels, with pairs of semicircles at the base to represent feet. On each side of the figures stands what looks like a rearing beast, also reduced to the simplest of lines—rather like the animals found in Scotland on the Pictish symbol-stones.

Composite scenes, like individual figures, were presented symbolically. The two main types of scene found on the Welsh monuments are biblical or other religious scenes, and the so-called 'hunting scenes' which depict warriors or huntsmen. The most common religious scene on the Celtic crosses was the Crucifixion itself, of which seven or eight examples have been identified by Nash-Williams on Welsh monuments. At Llanychaer in Pembrokeshire,[32] for instance, a four-sided stone pillar bears crosses in different styles on each of its four faces: on the fourth face it is the outstretched figure of Christ himself that forms the cross. He is shown as a bearded figure, staring straight ahead, with a nimbus encircling his head and a long-sleeved garment covering his body. This is the Byzantine conception of Christ (quite different from the naked, clean-shaven Christ of Roman and Hellenistic tradition, who also appears on some Welsh monuments). Similar depictions are found in Coptic icons and textiles of sixth- to seventh-century date, and some such portable material, brought by trading-vessels to the western British coast, must surely have been the craftsman's source. Sometimes onlookers and attendants were included in the Crucifixion scenes: a fine tenth- or eleventh-century example on a monument at Llangan in Glamorgan[33] shows a large figure of Christ, filling the head of the cross, flanked by the sponge-bearer and spear-bearer, who are suitably diminutive in comparison. Occasionally only the onlookers appear, while the cross alone represents the crucified Christ: an example can be seen on a damaged stone slab at Llanhamlach in Breconshire.[34] The slab is covered with a profusion of symbols, but central to the design is a cross, with a robed figure standing to each side of it, their arms raised in prayer; circles representing breasts identify the right-hand figure as female. The figures are thought to be St John and the Virgin, standing at the foot of the cross: the lance-bearer and the sponge-bearer were the traditional attendants in Irish and Hiberno-Saxon crucifixion scenes, but St John and the Virgin appear in English depictions contemporary with the tenth- or eleventh-century Llanhamlach slab. The lack of perspective in all these scenes, of any attempt to relate the figures to a background, is too easily dismissed as 'primitive': for the Celtic craftsman it was the association of symbols (including human figures), not any concern with spatial relationships, that comprised a scene. One great advantage of this approach was that groups of symbols could stand for the whole of an event—for everything that happened at the Crucifixion—whereas representational scenes have the same limitations as photographs: they can capture only one second in time.

The scenes of warriors and huntsmen beloved of the Celtic artists may derive from some influential Celtic myth or legend. Hunting scenes also played a significant role in early Celtic literature: the boar-hunt in the early Arthurian tale of *Culhwch ac Olwen* is an entertaining example. Just as legends and myths could be 'Arthurianized', so they could be Christianized. Christianity was already steeped in battle-imagery. Armed figures on the Christian monuments (like the engaging warrior on a stone slab at Eglwysilan in Glamorgan,[35] prancing with a shield clutched in one hand and a sword strapped to his waist) may be close in style to pagan art, but in Christian times they may well have been used to represent some Christian figure, such as a saint engaged in the battle against evil.

Glamorgan was an important centre of production of the late, sculpted crosses, though it is not particularly rich in monuments of earlier date. This rise to prominence as a centre of stone-carving is especially interesting, since it confirms the evidence of the saints' *Lives* and the *Book of Llandaff* that on the eve of the Norman arrival in Wales the churches of Glamorgan were wealthy and influential establishments, building up their power within the Church in Wales, a process which was to culminate in the founding of the see of Llandaff and its ambitious claims to authority. Today, a good selection of these Glamorgan monuments can be seen in the Margam Stones Museum: they are rather heavy sculptures, with large cross-heads supported by short, squat stems, often set on bulky pedestals. But if they are less elegant than the tall, slender crosses found for instance at Penmon, Anglesey, and at several sites in Pembrokeshire, they are undoubtedly impressive. Some of them bear unusually elaborate inscriptions. Elsewhere, the inscriptions on the crosses remain simple in form: typically '*x* built this cross'. But in Glamorgan lengthy inscriptions occur on some monuments, drawing heavily on phrases, abbreviations, and other features from contemporary manuscript usage. For example, at Llantwit Major a cross-shaft bears twenty-two lines of rather untidy lettering, recording that the cross was set up by Abbot Samson for his own soul and for the soul of King Juthahel and other persons.[36]

It may be that originally the inscriptions and perhaps the decoration on the crosses were picked out with coloured pigment. A unique inscription on the stone called Eliseg's Pillar, in Denbighshire,[37] celebrates the ancestors of King Concenn of Powys and their achievements: at the end of the inscription it is said that 'Conmarch painted this writing . . .' When one of the stones at Llantwit Major was cleaned at the end of the last century there were thought to be signs that the inscription had been painted black at some date.[38]

The tradition of stone-carving was deeply enough entrenched in Wales to influence for some time the ecclesiastical sculpture of the Norman-controlled, medieval Church. The early medieval fonts, grave-slabs, churchyard crosses, and so on often bear inscriptions or decoration in Celtic style. Most of these monuments are to be found in Glamorgan and Anglesey, which had been among the centres of stone-carving in the late days of the Celtic Church: presumably the old craftsmen and their pupils were now working for new masters. At Coychurch in Glamorgan[39] there is a damaged eleventh- or twelfth-century cross, much like any other medieval churchyard cross, except that it is decorated all over in purely Celtic idiom. A twelfth-century tub-shaped font at Newborough, Anglesey,[40] bears three panels of deeply cut, maze-like designs; while another font, at Partrishow in Breconshire,[41] bears an inscription on its rim in the old Hiberno-Saxon rounded script, declaring that 'Menhir made me in the time of Genillin'.

But the days of the old fashions were numbered. At Llanfihangel-y-traethau in Merioneth[42] is a mid-twelfth-century monument that shows clearly the shape of things to come. The church beside which the monument stands is spectacularly sited on a hillock that until about 200 years ago was an island in the estuary overlooked by Porthmadoc and Harlech. The site was chosen not because of the wonderful views of the surrounding water and mountains, but because, like St Michael's Mount in Cornwall, it was a suitable position for a church dedicated to St Michael (who was supposed to have appeared in a vision on a mountain-top). St Michael's cult was fashionable in the twelfth century, and here we can see how, via the Normans, the fashion had spread to Wales. The stone monument records the grave of the mother of the church's founder, and dates the foundation to the reign of Owain Gwynedd (ruled 1137–70). This inscription is not in the rounded Celtic lettering, but in the angular, continental script: already Norman influence was sufficiently strong to have displaced one of the most basic features of Celtic Christian culture.

Yet however much the Normans extinguished Celtic individuality, some traditions from the days of the Celtic Church have survived. An amusing example of continuity is a monument in the church at Steynton, Pembrokeshire.[43] Originally this stone was inscribed in Ogam and Latin in the early days of the church; much later, in the tenth or eleventh century, a cross was added. After another long interval, a panel was inscribed below the cross, and an epitaph written to one T. Harries, who died in January 1876. Remembering how the Celtic Christians were quite happy to re-use Roman stones for their monuments (for example, an altar at Loughor, Glamorgan,[44] and a milestone at Port Talbot[45]), I cannot help suspecting that they would have had more sympathy with this expedient use of their work than with our modern custom of isolating monuments in museums. However interesting and beautiful in their own right are the manuscripts and monuments which the Celtic Church has bequeathed to us, we should not forget that the Church's primary concern was not with material excellence, but with men's souls.

Notes

CHAPTER 1

1 At this date, *Scotti* (Scots) denoted the Irish; their settlements in the west of modern Scotland were ultimately to gain control over the whole of the area to which they gave their name, which had previously been controlled by the Picts.

2 Of course, if these martyrs were soldiers, they were quite probably not of British descent.

3 Until recently, much work on the Celtic Church has lacked the all-important element of historical perspective. Saints' *Lives* were dismissed as superstitious fabrications. The cult of relics seemed distasteful to writers influenced by later religious controversies. Crude images on some of the inscribed stones were ignored. Then the Church, shorn of its native colouring and primitive vigour, was pictured as an idealistic institution, staffed by dedicated holy men—the Celtic saints. To see the Church in that way is to forget that it was rooted in a society which was, by our standards, primitive, violent, and harsh.

4 i.e. paganism as a total system of belief. Remnants of paganism—myths, superstitions, spells, etc.—survived much longer, some up to the present day.

5 For the long-lived importance of the Irish Sea in facilitating cultural contact between the inhabitants of its shores, see *The Irish Sea Province in Archaeology and History*, ed. D. Moore, Cambrian Archaeological Association (Cardiff 1970).

6 N–W Nos. 91 and 103.

7 Ed. H. Williams, *De Excidio Britanniae . . .*, Cymmrodorion Record Series No. 3 (London 1899–1901).

8 The process by which the Church in another Celtic land, Ireland, became integrated into society is traced by K. Hughes, *The Church in Early Irish Society* (London 1966). Sadly, there is insufficient evidence from Wales to permit so detailed a study.

9 Pelagius, originator of the heresy, was himself of British descent. After prolonged controversy, his denial of the doctrine of divine grace in favour of freewill to do God's purpose was condemned as heresy in A.D. 418; but his ideas long remained influential.

10 There is no evidence that the British were such inveterate wanderers as the Irish, many of whom went into voluntary exile in their restless search for

God, sometimes making an important contribution to the life of the continental Church. St Columbanus, for instance, in the sixth century founded monasteries in Gaul and Italy. But the distribution of the cults of the Welsh saints shows that they or their followers did travel, at least within the Celtic lands; while Gildas quite casually mentions that candidates would go to Gaul to obtain ordination as bishops, if they were refused it at home.

11 Canon 33 of the so-called First Synod of St Patrick decreed that a cleric from Britain without an authorizing letter was not to minister.

12 Except to St Brigid; but there was a resurgence of her cult in the eleventh century, and many of the dedications may date from then.

13 Bede, *Ecclesiastical History*, I. 27.

14 The Irish, relatively safe from the Anglo-Saxon threat, made an important contribution to their conversion.

15 The Dyke has been studied in detail by Sir Cyril Fox, *Offa's Dyke, a Field Survey* . . . (Cardiff 1955).

16 Even the renowned poet, Sedulius Scottus, an Irishman who had settled in the land of the Franks, was apparently inspired to address a panegyric to Rhodri: see N. K. Chadwick, *Studies in the Early British Church* (Cambridge 1938), pp. 83–118.

17 There is no early evidence that St Germanus, on his visits to Britain to crush the Pelagian heresy, ever penetrated as far west as Powys. The later traditions connecting him with the area may be the result of confusion with a local saint, Garmon.

18 The Latin text of Asser's *Life* is edited by W. H. Stevenson; new impression, with article by D. Whitelock (Oxford 1959). There is an English translation in J. A. Giles, *Six Old English Chronicles* (London 1868).

19 Ed. Sir I. Williams (Cardiff 1955).

20 The ways in which the beliefs and practice of the Celtic churches differed from Roman usage are discussed by L. Hardinge, *The Celtic Church in Britain* (London 1972): but most of the evidence is from Ireland.

21 Despite later claims that the see was founded by St Kentigern: see K. H. Jackson, 'The Sources for the Life of St Kentigern', in *Studies in the Early British Church*, ed. N. K. Chadwick (Cambridge 1958), pp. 273–357.

CHAPTER 2

1 For the meaning of *Merthyr* in place-names, see below, p. 30–1. The relationship of Celtic church sites to topography is discussed by E. G. Bowen, *The Settlements of the Celtic Saints in Wales* (Cardiff 1956), Part II.

2 For Ireland, a similar view is convincingly argued by Dr K. Hughes in *The Modern Traveller to the Early Irish Church* (London 1976).

3 See C. Thomas, *Britain and Ireland in Early Christian Times* (London 1971), pp. 109ff.

4 The same sequence has been identified on a site on Church Island in S.W. Ireland.

5 Since stone monuments can be moved and dedications changed, these last two types of evidence in particular need to be considered with care.

6 Examples are given by Bowen, *The Settlements of the Celtic Saints in Wales*, p. 104, n.1.

7 The Celtic church could not, of course, copy cremation, since resurrection of the body was taken literally.

8 At Maughold, in the Isle of Man, a Celtic monastery was actually provided with a piped water supply: a memorial stone, dated to *c*.A.D. 800, commemorates 'Branhui who led off water to this place', and the remains of a stone-lined conduit have been found (see N. K. Chadwick, *Celtic Britain* (London 1963), p. 227).

9 From Irish *ráth*, ring-fort. This type of homestead is thought to have been introduced by Irish settlers.

10 Sometimes Celtic monasteries were founded within existing strongholds: Tintagel, in Cornwall, lies within a promontory fort, and several of the Irish Saints' *Lives* tell how the local chieftain handed over his *dun* (fortified homestead) for the use of the saint. But in Wales, E. G. Bowen states: 'there is not a single well-authenticated instance of a Celtic church established within the defences of a native hill-fort or Dark Age fortified homestead.' (*The Settlements of the Celtic Saints in Wales*, p. 120). There is, however, some evidence for re-use of Roman sites: see below, pp. 42–3.

11 Num. 35., 10–12. See Hardinge, *The Celtic Church in Britain* (London 1972), pp. 173ff. The granting of sanctuary is discussed below, pp. 85–7.

12 In *A Hundred Years of Welsh Archaeology*, ed. V. E. Nash-Williams (Gloucester 1946), p. 111.

13 See Thomas, *Britain and Ireland*, p. 119.

14 'The church of the grave', built to house the tomb of St Beuno.

15 The markers were inserted after the excavation of the remains in 1913. The building measured *c*.18 × 9.75 feet.

16 'Seiriol's island', where Seiriol was believed to have been buried. The Vikings, who raided Penmon and Ynys Seiriol during their frequent attacks on Anglesey in the tenth century, called the island 'Priestholme'; today the English name, 'Puffin Island', seems more appropriate.

17 See Hardinge, *The Celtic Church in Britain*, pp. 169ff.

18 For married clergy and monks, see below, pp. 56–8.

19 Centuries later, St Cadog's biographer was so impressed by Llancarfan's position as a focus of routes, that he credited the saint, when founding the site, with making 'four large foot-paths across four declivities of mountains surrounding his monastery' (*Life of St Cadog*, para. 9).

20 See Bowen, *The Settlements of the Celtic Saints in Wales*, p. 45.

21 See Owen Chadwick, 'The Evidence of Dedications in the Early History of the Welsh Church', in *Studies in Early British History*, ed. N. K. Chadwick (Cambridge 1954). He suggests that the formal dedications date from the seventh to eighth centuries.

22 Even in the Irish-settled areas of Wales, where Ogam inscriptions are found (in the Goidelic speech), it is the Brittonic forms of the saints' names that have been preserved.

23 See G. H. Doble, *Saint Patern*. Cornish Saints' Series, No. 43, 1940.

24 The *Life of St Samson*, thought to be based on an early seventh-century *Life*, is the only exception to the rule that the existing *Lives* of the Welsh saints were written five centuries or so after their subjects' lifetimes. They are more valuable as evidence for the Church at the time they were written than as evidence for the Church in the age of the saints.

25 *The Settlements of the Celtic Saints in Wales*, p. 53.

26 See Bowen, *The Settlements of the Celtic Saints in Wales*, pp. 106–7.

27 These monuments comprise Group I in Nash-Williams's classification.

28 N–W No. 229. Now in the Margam Stones Museum.

29 Matt. 23.9: this explanation is proposed by Nash-Williams, following a suggestion by Le Blant.

30 N–W No. 32. Inside the church, built into the chancel wall.

31 *Britain and Ireland in Early Christian Times*, p. 106.

32 N–W No. 87. Built into the west wall of the church's north transept.

33 Modern curraghs are covered with calico and flannel, not skins, and can carry up to ten men. The following account of British navigation is based on that of E. G. Bowen in *Britain and the Western Seaways* (London 1972), a book that traces the history of the western British sea-routes from prehistoric times up to the present day.

34 ibid. p. 37.

35 N–W No. 90.

36 Sails may sometimes have been used in the skin boats, as in modern curraghs: for instance, a boat with a sail is mentioned in the seventh-century Life of the Irish saint, Columba.

37 The story is designed to explain the name of Barry Island, supposedly named after Barruc, one of the drowned disciples.

38 This is an eighteenth-century description, by Archdeacon Edward Yardley (in *Menevia Sacra*); but pilgrims had travelled to St David's by sea for centuries.

39 See Bowen, *The Settlements of the Celtic Saints in Wales*, pp. 74ff.

40 This can be seen by correlating the distribution-patterns of Celtic dedications and inscribed stones with the pattern of the Roman roads: see Bowen, pp. 24–32.

41 N–W No. 73. See Plate I(a).

42 Of course, few of the passers-by would themselves be able to read the inscription: literacy was the prerogative of an élite.

43 N–W No. 258. Now in the Margam Stones Museum.

44 *Life of St Samson*, ch. 40 and 41.

45 e.g. the dedication to the Trinity, a dedication made popular by the Normans.

46 *Ecclesiastical History*, III. 23.

CHAPTER 3

1 Ariconium was near Ross-on-Wye; later, Erging became the Archenfield Hundred of Hereford.

2 N–W, chart on p. 2. The few monuments found in Archenfield are almost all of ninth-century or later date.

3 Ed. L. Bieler, *The Works of St. Patrick* (London 1953).

4 N–W No. 33. In the grounds of Trescawen house.

5 The Paulinus mentioned could be the saint Paulinus who reputedly taught St David, and who may well be the Paulinus celebrated in verse as 'Preserver of the faith, constant lover of his country ... devout champion of righteousness' on a stone from Cynwyl Gaeo, Carmarthenshire (N–W No. 139. Now in Carmarthen Museum).

6 N–W No. 83. The word used here and in the Llantrisant inscription is *sacerdos*, which in the fourth and fifth centuries can usually be translated as 'bishop', though later it came to mean 'priest'. The Bodafon stone is mounted in the south wall of Llanrhos church.

7 N–W Nos. 77 and 78.

8 N–W No. 91. In the churchyard.

9 N–W No. 103. Inside the church at Penmachno, Caernarvonshire.

10 N–W No. 78.

11 The rules followed in Brittany and Scotland are also unknown to us; and from Ireland we have only the Rule of Ailbe—not in its original form—and the rule imposed by the Irish St Columbanus in his foundations on the Continent. Both of these impose a severe ascetic regime.

12 *Ecclesiastical History*, II. iii.

13 Chs. 21–31. This section differs little in the two chief versions of the *Life*, the Nero and Vespasian recensions, suggesting that the revisers of the *Life* had special respect for its authenticity.

14 Contact between St David's and the leaders of the Irish ascetic revival is attested by the inclusion in a calendar of saints drawn up by the revivers (The Calendar of Oengus, *c.*A.D. 800) of 'David Cille Mune' ('Cille Mune' = Menevia, the old name of St David's). This is probably the earliest known reference to the saint.

15 This nickname can be traced back to the ninth century, when it occurs in the Breton *Life of St Paul Aurelian*.

16 N–W Nos. 220–6.

17 See above, p. 8. Later writers, including the author of the *Life of St Illtud*, say that St Dubricius ordained St Illtud: but they were influenced by Llandaff's propagandist revival of Dubricius's cult.

18 *Ecclesiastical History*, II. iii.

19 K. Hughes, O'Donnell Lecture (Oxford 1975).

20 The rivalries between the major churches in South Wales, especially be-
    tween St David's and Llancarfan (whose clerics played a leading part in the
    foundation in the early twelfth century of the see of Llandaff), and the
    development of metropolitan claims are studied by C. N. L. Brooke, 'The
    Archbishops of St. David's, Llandaff and Caerleon-on-Usk', in *Studies in
    the Early British Church*, ed. N. K. Chadwick *et al.* (Cambridge 1958), and
    'St. Peter of Gloucester and St. Cadoc of Llancarfan', in *Celt and Saxon*,
    ed. N. K. Chadwick *et al* (Cambridge 1963).

21 The form of haircut or tonsure used by the Celtic clergy and monks to
    distinguish themselves from laymen is uncertain. Bede (*Ecclesiastical
    History*, V. 21) said it looked like a crown from the front, but the crown was
    not continued at the back. It may have resembled the way the druids
    (known by the Christians as magicians, or *magi*) cut their hair, which would
    explain why its opponents condemned it as the tonsure of Simon the
    Magician (Simon Magus).

22 *De Excidio*, ch. cix.

23 N–W No. 33.

24 N–W No. 32. Built into the N. chancel wall of Llansadwrn church. The
    adjective *beatus* suggests Saturninus was a bishop, since in early epitaphs it
    is normally used only of bishops, martyrs, or confessors.

25 The story-cycle from which the collection of tales known as the *Mabinogion*
    takes its name. Trans. with Introduction by G. Jones and T. Jones, *The
    Mabinogian* (Everyman's Library, London 1949, repr. 1966).

26 See Hughes, *The Church in Early Irish Society*, pp. 76–7.

27 In Ireland, the incidence of filial succession and pluralism and the tenure
    by laymen of church appointments is known to have increased as a result of
    the disruption caused by the Vikings: see Hughes, *The Church in Early
    Irish Society*, ch. 19.

28 Melville Richards, *The Laws of Hywel Dda* (The Book of Blegywryd)
    (Liverpool 1954), p. 105.

29 A. W. Wade-Evans, *Welsh Medieval Law* (Oxford 1909), p. 208.

30 Scotland and Ireland had their own versions of this legend. Merfyn was
    originally a North British hero.

31 N–W No. 250.

CHAPTER 4

1 See N. K. Chadwick, *Celtic Britain*, p. 113.

2 From the Anglo-Saxon kingdoms, whose conversion is better recorded than
   that of the Celtic lands, we have examples of kings expelling missionaries
   (e.g. in Essex), while others (like Raedwald of East Anglia, who set up an
   altar to Christ alongside altars to pagan gods) put their own interpretation
   upon the new faith.

3   H. Trevor-Roper, *The Rise of Christian Europe* (Norwich 1965), p. 100.

4   *Life of Alfred*, ch. 79.

5   See Chadwick, *Celtic Britain*, esp. p. 70, and the note on p. 223 referring to Plate 16, for this and other examples of churches near courts.

6   N–W No. 13.

7   *The Early Christian Monuments of Wales*, p. 57.

8   N–W No. 220. Now in the church.

9   N–W No. 222. Also in the church.

10 N–W No. 223. In the churchyard. It is interesting that the names Samson and Illtud recur in these inscriptions: presumably the families connected with the church were naming their children in honour of its patron, St Illtud, and his famous pupil. The description in the *Life of St Illtud* of St Samson's grave (para. 15) could be the result of confusion between the saint and his namesake on one of these ninth- or tenth-century crosses.

11 For the rite of baptism in the Celtic churches, see Hardinge, *The Celtic Church in Britain*, pp. 101ff.

12 Trans. K. H. Jackson (Edinburgh 1969).

13 It has recently been suggested by Dr K. W. Hughes that the severe sexual restrictions imposed on laymen in the penitentials may have been aimed not at ordinary laymen, but at the *manaig* (monastic clients), who lived with their families on the monastic estates. (Unpublished.)

14 N–W No. 62. At Llanlleonfel.

15 Following the interpretation of Sir I. Williams, 'An Old Welsh Verse', *National Library of Wales Journal*, II (1941–2), pp. 69–75.

16 Edited and translated by Sir I. Williams, art.cit. The four-line verse is written on fol.11 of Corpus Christi MS.199, written by Sulien's son, Ieuan, in *c.*1080–90.

17 i.e. from the period with which we are concerned: saints' *Lives* written in Welsh survive from a later date.

18 See Plate IV(b).

19 'The Book of the Angel', translated as Appendix in Hughes, *The Church in Early Irish Society*.

20 Ch. 57: found only in the Vespasian recension of the Life, for the late date of which see James, *Rhigyfarch's Life of St David*, pp. xxivff.

21 *Life of St Cadog*, para. 33: see above, p. 84.

CHAPTER 5

1   N–W No. 124.

2   N–W No. 255: now in the National Museum of Wales, Cardiff.

3   N–W No. 240.

4   See Hardinge, *The Celtic Church in Britain*, pp. 161ff.

5   *Description of Wales*, ch. xviii.

6 See Frank R. Lewis, 'The Racial Sympathies of the Welsh Cistercians', *Transactions of the Honourable Society of the Cymmrodorion*, 1938.

CHAPTER 6

1 For the development of the British languages, see K. H. Jackson, *Language and History in Early Britain* (Edinburgh 1953).

2 C. Mohrmann, *The Latin of St. Patrick* (Dublin 1961).

3 See Chadwick, *Celtic Britain*, p. 117.

4 A key to the Ogam alphabet is printed in *The Irish Sea Province in Archaeology and History*, ed. D. Moore (Cardiff 1970), p. 59.

5 N–W No. 287.

6 There are also two later additions to the inscription.

7 The triads served as a sort of index to the characters of native tradition: see R. Bromwich, *Trioedd Ynys Prydain* (Cardiff 1961).

8 For this and other contributions of the Celtic church in Ireland to medieval Christianity, see L. Bieler, *Ireland, Harbinger of the Middle Ages* (London 1963).

9 J. E. Caerwyn Williams, 'Bucheddau'r Saint', *Bulletin of the Board of Celtic Studies*, XI (1944), Pts. iii and iv.

10 Detailed analysis of the *Life of St Cadog* by Dr H. D. Emmanuel has shown that it was altered and expanded in several stages after Lifris had written the basic text ('The Latin Life of St Cadoc: a Textual and Lexicographical Study', M.A. thesis, Aberystwyth 1950).

11 The following account of the Welsh annals is based on the study by K. Hughes, *The Welsh Latin Chronicles: 'Annales Cambriae' and Related Texts*, Sir John Rhys Memorial Lecture (British Academy 1973).

12 'Annales Cambriae', ed. E. Phillimore, *Y Cymmrodor*, IX (1888), pp. 141–84.

13 The version in Peniarth MS.20 is edited by T. Jones, *Brut y Tywysogyon* (Cardiff 1956).

14 *Concenn* is probably Cyngen, King of Powys at this time.

15 The claim is made in a note in an early-ninth-century manuscript, the copy of the *Liber Commonei* in MS. Oxoniensis Prior.

16 See Sir J. E. Lloyd, *A History of Wales* (London 1954), pp. 459–61.

17 The poem is written, perhaps in Rhigyfarch's own hand, in the copy of the Psalter made for Rhigyfarch (Trinity College, Dublin, MS.A.4.20).

18 Their achievements are discussed in two essays by C. N. L. Brooke, cited above in Chapter 3, n. 20.

19 The hybrid culture developed in Northumbria and other areas of England where the influence of Irish missionaries was strong.

20 N–W No. 13: see also pp. 68–9, above.

21 The manuscript is described and discussed by F. Henry, in *Irish Art in the*

Early Christian Period to A.D. 800 (London 1965), pp. 183ff., where several folios from the manuscript are reproduced in colour and monochrome.

22 Ibid. pp. 186 and 195.

23 N–W No. 27: now in the Museum of the University College at Bangor.

24 N–W No. 71.

25 See Henry, *Irish Art in the Early Christian Period*, p. 204.

26 The 'panelled-cartwheel' cross-slabs, of which eleven examples are catalogued by Nash-Williams.

27 N–W No. 236. Now in the Margam Stones Museum.

28 A most illuminating account of the meaning, aims, and methods of Celtic art is given by F. Henry in Chapter 8 of *Irish Art in the Early Christian Period*.

29 N–W No. 256. Built into the outside wall of the chapel.

30 N–W No. 269.

31 N–W No. 218. In the churchyard.

32 N–W No. 337.

33 N–W No. 207. In the churchyard.

34 N–W No. 61. Inside the church, tucked away behind the pews facing the doorway. See Plate I (b).

35 N–W No. 195. In the church.

36 See above, p. 69.

37 N–W No. 182. The monument was broken during the Civil War, but has been re-erected on its original site near Valle Crucis Abbey, near Glamorgan.

38 N–W No. 222.

39 N–W No. 194. The broken fragments of the cross are inside the church.

40 N–W No. 36. See Plate III (a).

41 N–W No. 67.

42 N–W No. 281. In the churchyard, facing the church doorway. See Plate III (b).

43 N–W No. 404.

44 N–W No. 228. In the grounds of the rectory.

45 N–W No. 258. In the Margam Stones Museum.

Suggestions for Further Reading

BARLEY, M. W., and HANSON, R.P.C. *Christianity in Britain 300–700.* Leicester 1968.

BIELER, L., *The Works of St Patrick.* Ancient Christian Writers No. 17, Westminster, Maryland 1953.

BOWEN, E. G., *Saints, Seaways and Settlements in the Celtic Lands.* Cardiff 1969.

BOWEN, E. G., *The Settlements of the Celtic Saints in Wales.* Cardiff 1956.

CHADWICK, N. K., *Celtic Britain.* London 1963.

CHADWICK, N. K., ed., *Studies in the Early British Church.* Cambridge 1958.

DOBLE, Canon G. H., *Saint Iltut.* Cardiff 1944.

DOBLE, Canon G. H., *Lives of the Welsh Saints*, ed. D. Simon Evans. Cardiff 1971.

GOUGAUD, L., *Christianity in Celtic Lands*, trans. M. Joynt. London 1932.

HARDINGE, L., *The Celtic Church in Britain.* London 1972.

HENRY, F., *Irish Art in the Early Christian Period to A.D. 800.* London 1965.

HENRY, F., *Irish Art during the Viking Invasions, 800–1020 A.D.* London 1965.

H.M.S.O., *Ancient Monuments of Wales.* London 1973.

HUGHES, K. W., *The Church in Early Irish Society.* London 1966.

JAMES, J. W., ed., *Rhigyfarch's Life of St. David.* Cardiff 1967.

JONES, F., *The Holy Wells of Wales.* Cardiff 1954.

JONES, G., *A History of the Vikings.* London 1968.

LLOYD, J. E., *History of Wales*, vol. I. London 1954.

McNeill, J. T., *The Celtic Churches*. Chicago and London 1974.

Nash-Williams, V. E., *The Early Christian Monuments of Wales*. Cardiff 1950.

Richards, M., *The Laws of Hywel Dda*, translated from the Book of Blegywryd. Liverpool 1954.

Thomas, C., *Britain and Ireland in Early Christian Times*. London 1971.

Wade-Evans, A. W., ed., *Vitae Sanctorum Britanniae et Genealogiae*. Cardiff 1944.

Williams, G., *The Welsh Church from Conquest to Reformation*. Cardiff 1962.

Suggestions for Places to Visit

NORTH-WEST WALES

Anglesey

Cerrig Ceinwen (twelfth-century font and cross-inscribed stones inside church)

Llangadwaladr (inscribed stone inside church)

Llansadwrn (inscribed stone inside church)

Penmon (stone cross and font inside church; holy well and stone cross nearby in Deer Park)

Caernarvonshire

Llanelhaiarn (inscribed stone inside church)

Llangian (inscribed stone in churchyard)

Llangybi (St Cybi's well, to rear of church)

Penmachno (inscribed stones inside church)

Merioneth

Llanfihangel-y-traethau (inscribed stone in churchyard)

SOUTH-WEST WALES

Cardiganshire

Llanbadarn-fawr (stone crosses inside church)

Carmarthenshire

Carmarthen Museum (inscribed stones etc.)

Pembrokeshire

Carew (stone cross at roadside)

Nevern (inscribed stones and crosses, in church and churchyard)

Penally (stone crosses in churchyard)

St David's (stone monuments dating from the fifth to the twelfth century, collected inside the cathedral)

St Dogmael's (stone monuments among the Abbey ruins and inside the church)

St Non's chapel and well (on the cliffs, south of St David's)

ELSEWHERE

Breconshire

Brecon Museum

Maen Madoc (beside the Roman road, near Ystradfellte)

Denbighshire

Eliseg's Pillar (at Llantysilio-yn-îal, by the site of Valle Crucis Abbey)

Glamorganshire

Cardiff, National Museum of Wales

Llantwit Major (stone crosses in church and churchyard)

Margam Stones Museum

Montgomeryshire

Meifod (cross-slab, inside church)

NOTE

This list is highly selective; many other sites will be found mentioned in the text.

Index

Aberdaron 47, 49
Aberffraw 68
Aidan, St (of Ferns) 33, 108
Alfred, King of England 3, 16–17, 66, 100, 102
altars 23, 76–7, 80, 83
anchorites 25, 61–2, 94; *see also* hermits
Anglo-Saxons 6, 8, 10–18, 37, 64, 66n, 71–2, 102, 114, 123
Anthony, St 50, 63
archbishop, in Wales 20, 55
Ardwall Isle 24, 76, 80
Arthur 35, 66, 86, 111–12, 117–18, 127
asceticism 32, 50–2, 56, 61–3, 79, 93
Asser 3, 17, 55, 66, 100, 102
Athelstan, King of England 18, 94
Augustine, St 11–12, 24, 62–3
Augustine of Hippo, St 56, 116, 120

Bangor 20
Bangor-is-coed 51–2, 54, 62
baptism 11, 23, 65, 70
bards 15, 38, 49, 78, 102–3, 108
Bardsey Island 18, 40, 82, 88
Barry Island 40, 54, 62
Bede 11–12, 43, 51–2, 54, 56n, 113
bells 76–8, 84–5
Bernard, Bp of St David's 20, 55, 116
Beuno, St 28
bishops: British 2–5, 11; in Wales 20, 45–7, 54–6, 66–7
Black Book of Carmarthen 103, 106
boats 39–40
Bodafon 47
Book of Kells 119
Book of Lichfield 3, 54–5, 57, 79, 105, 119–20
Book of Lindisfarne 119

Book of Llandaff 3–4, 54, 82–3, 111, 117, 127
Book of Mulling 124
Brittany 10, 14, 33–5, 39, 41, 51n, 52, 68, 81, 99, 111, 121
Brynach, St 31–2, 97–8
burial-grounds *see* cemeteries
Byzantium 13, 43, 69, 126

Cadfan, King of Gwynedd 68, 119
Cadog, St 41, 60, 62, 70–5, 77, 81–7, 90, 94–5, 97–8, 107, 109–10, 112–13, 117
Cadwallon, King of Gwynedd 13, 68
Caergybi 33–4, 40, 42
Caerleon 2
Caerwent 2, 6, 43
Caldey Island 18, 31, 40
Caradoc of Llancarfan 117–18
Cassian, John 50, 70–1
Cassiodorus 51, 79
celibacy *see* clergy, married; children, of ecclesiastics
cemeteries 23–7, 37–8, 60, 74–6
chapels *see* sites, of chapels etc.
children, of ecclesiastics 30, 56–61
Cistercians 21, 99, 113
clasau 20–1, 54, 60–1
clergy, married 56–8
clergy, status of 46–9, 52, 61, 78, 94
Clynnog Fawr 25, 27–8, 88, 114
Columbanus, St 9n, 51n, 52, 71
Concenn (Cyngen), King of Powys 114, 128
confession 70–2, 96
confessors *see* confession
Cornwall 10, 14, 34–9, 41
Coroticus 48, 66
courts, ecclesiastical 55, 72–3, 81, 86
Coychurch 128

crosses *see* monuments, Christian stone

Crucifixion scenes 126–7

Cunedda 10, 41

Cybi, St 33–5, 40–1, 44, 79, 107

Cydifor, grandson of Sulien 116

Cynwyl Gaeo 47n

Daniel, son of Sulien 116

David, St 34–5, 47n, 52, 76, 78–9, 81, 86, 95, 98, 107–10, 113, 115

dedications, of churches *see* saints, cults of

diet 93–5

dioceses, Welsh 20–1, 45–6, 54–5, 86

Dol 81, 111

druids 38, 48, 56n, 71

Dubricius, St 33, 45–6, 53n, 54, 82

Dyfrig, St *see* Dubricius, St

Easter, controversy over date 11, 15, 20, 55–6, 80

education 29, 46–7, 51, 53, 59–61, 65, 70, 90, 101–2, 106–9

Edward the Elder, King of England 17–18

Eglwysilan 127

Elfoddw, Bp of Gwynedd 15, 55

'Eliseg's Pillar' 128

enclosures, religious *see* sites, of chapels etc.

endowments 52, 89–91

fonts 128–9

Gaul 7, 9–12, 37, 45–7, 50–1, 57–8, 80, 118

genealogies 10, 15, 36, 101, 112–13

Germanus, Bp of Auxerre 8, 16, 53, 95

Gildas 3, 7–10, 16, 37–8, 43, 45, 48–9, 51, 53, 57, 64–6, 71, 77, 84, 93, 95, 97, 100–1, 103, 108, 110

Giraldus Cambrensis 22, 61, 77–8, 88, 91, 95

Glascwm 78

Gospel books 76, 78–9, 84–6, 92, 119–20

Gospels of St Chad *see Book of Lichfield*

Gruffydd ap Cynan 66–7, 115

Gwenfrewi, St 58, 79

Gwynllyw, St 67, 70, 75, 82, 87, 92, 94, 112

Harold, King of England 67, 87

Hastings, Battle of 19, 67, 87

Hemeid, King of Dyfed 17, 66–7

Henry, grandson of Sulien 116

hermitages 29, 31, 40

hermits 30–1, 62–3; *see also* anchorites

Holyhead *see* Caergybi

Holywell (St Winifred's Well) 58, 79

hospitality 38, 96–9

Hywel Dda 17–18, 72

Ieuan, son of Sulien 19, 78n, 106, 115–16, 120

Illtud, St 24, 32–4, 52–3, 58–9, 67, 69n, 73, 77, 81, 85, 87, 93, 98, 108

inheritance: laws of 16, 60, 90; of ecclesiastical posts 56–7, 59–61, 70

Ireland 10, 34, 39–40, 47, 77, 95, 104–5, 107, 114

Irish Church 37, 44, 52–4, 80, 110, 114

Irish settlement in Wales 5, 10, 41

Isle of Man 18, 25n, 40

Ithael 110, 116

Jerusalem 34; Patriarch of 76, 78

Latin 6, 10, 15, 46–7, 59, 64–5, 100–5, 107–9, 111

Laws, Welsh 18, 55, 61, 72, 92, 94, 103

Lent 43, 62, 112

Lifris 106, 112, 116–18

literacy 6, 15, 46–7, 70, 72, 92, 104, 106

liturgy 109–10

Lives of the Welsh saints 4, 19, 25, 34, 51, 55, 58, 60, 62, 65, 67–8, 76, 78, 80–1, 85, 88, 91, 93, 97–8, 106, 109–13, 115–16, 127

llan 23

Llanafan Fawr 30
Llanbadarn Fawr 35, 57, 68, 75, 78, 110, 115–16
Llancarfan 30, 56n, 62, 72–5, 77, 81, 83–7, 90–1, 97, 116–17
Llandaff 20, 30, 56n, 72, 78, 82–3, 111, 117–18, 127
Llanddewi Brefi 61, 122
Llandeilo Fawr 83, 119
Llanelhaiarn 38
Llanfaglan 39
Llanfihangel-y-traethau 129, Plate III(b)
Llangadwaladr 22, 68, 119
Llangan 126
Llangeinwen 120
Llangian 7, 47
Llangibby-on-Usk 34
Llangwnadl 77
Llangybi 34, 79–80, Plate IV(b)
Llanhamlach 126–7, Plate I(b)
Llanlleonfel 75n
Llanllyr 90
Llanrhidian 125
Llansadwrn 37, 57
Llantrisant 47, 57
Llantwit Major (Llanilltud) 22, 30, 32–3, 52–3, 69, 77, 81, 90–1, 93, 96, 128
Llanychaer 126
long-cist graves 25
Loughor 129
Loyngarth 76
Lydney, temple of Nodens 4–5

Mabinogion 58, 74, 112, 116
Madog, St 33
Maelgwn, King of Gwynedd 42, 49, 53, 65, 71, 97, 102, 108
Maen Madoc 42, Plate I(a)
manuscript production 94, 118–20
Margam 123–4, Plate II
martyrs, in Britain 2
Merfyn, King of Gwynedd 114–15
Merthyr Mawr 92, 123
Merthyr Tydfil 22, 31
metalwork 18, 100
miracle stories 25, 53, 79, 83–8
monasteries see sites, of chapels etc.

monasticism: Benedictine 50–1, 56; Celtic 9, 49–56, 62, 90–1, 106–7; origins 9, 49–50, 62
monuments, Christian stone: general 3, 24, 29, 36–7, 46, 48, 120–9; inscribed stones 7, 9–10, 36, 47, 49, 101–5, 118, 120–2; stone crosses 23, 37, 52, 55, 85, 92, 119, 122–8
Mynydd Illtud 24

Nash 63
Neath 123
Nennius 3, 15, 53, 77, 100, 102, 105–6, 114–15
Nevern 122
Newborough 128, Plate III(a)
Nobis, Bp of St David's 17, 55
Nobis, Bp of St Teilo 57
Nodens 4–5
Normans 19–22, 35, 55–6, 58, 61–2, 66–8, 72–4, 81–2, 86, 88–9, 91, 107, 111, 113, 115–18, 127, 129
numerical symbolism 109

oaths 84–5
Offa's Dyke 14–15
Ogam 10, 37, 104–5, 120–1, 129
Ogmore 92
oratories see sites, of chapels etc.
Oudoceus, St 78, 82–3
Owain Gwynedd 129

Padarn, St 33–4, 68, 75–6, 78, 81, 84–5, 91, 103, 106, 110
paganism 4–5, 24–6, 40, 64, 76, 102, 109, 125
parochial system 22–3, 45
Partrishow 22, 128, Cover, Plate IV(a)
Patrick, St 10, 32, 46–9, 56, 66, 101
Paul, St: teachings of 47, 57
Paulinus 47, 107, 109
Pelagian heresy 8, 53, 95
Penally 83
penance 12, 39, 66, 70–1, 73
penitentials 70–1
Penmachno 7, 48
Penmon 22, 28–9, 80, 123, 128
pilgrimages 74, 96
pilgrims 30, 83, 88

145

Pontardawe 125
Port Talbot 42, 129
pottery, imported 7–8, 37, 39, 95
Priestholm 18, 91
princes, British 7–8, 11, 17–18, 23, 60, 64–70, 76, 84, 88, 97, 101–2

relics 33, 76, 83–8; *see also* altars, bells, staffs, Gospel books; bodily relics 80–3
Rhigyfarch, son of Sulien 19, 32, 57, 76, 110, 115–16, 120
Rhodri, King of Gwynedd 15–17
Rhun ap Maelgwn 72, 94
Rhys ap Tewdwr 19, 115
Roman roads 41–2
Romans 1–9, 41–3, 45–8, 65, 100–2, 106–7, 121–2, 129
Rome 11, 21, 56, 72, 74, 80, 107

St Asaph 20
St David's 17–18, 20, 22, 32, 40, 55–7, 75–6, 86, 88, 95, 110, 115–16, 118, 123; chronicle kept at 3, 113; monastic rule of 51–2, 61, 89, 93, 96, 111
St Dogmael's 122
St Non's Well 80
St Peter's of Gloucester 20, 68, 117
St Woolo's 75
saints: cults of 9n, 10, 21, 24–5, 32–5, 39, 40–1, 74–88, 110–13; Irish 10
Samson, St 3, 34–5, 43, 58–60, 62, 69n
sanctuary 26, 85–7, 96
Sarn Helen 42
scribes 52, 109, 116
script, Celtic half-uncial 118–19, 129
Scriptures, study of 46, 53, 108–9

Seiriol, St 28–9, 80
Seven Sisters 125
Sicily 72, 81
sites: consecration of 43–4; of chapels, churches, monasteries, etc. 22–33, 40, 42–3, 68–9
slaves 16, 84
staffs 76, 78, 84–5, 103, 106
Stephen, brother of Lifris 117
Steynton 129
stone-carving 18, 69, 100
Strata Florida 21, 113
Sulien, Bp of St David's 115; family of 19, 57, 60, 115–16, 120
Sulien, son of Rhigyfarch 116
sundials 114

Tatheus, St 39, 43, 94
Teilo, St 55, 76, 78, 82–3, 103
Tintagel 26n, 27, 49, 51
tithing 95–6
tonsure 11, 56
Towyn 105
Trecastle 121
Trinihid 58–9, 98
Tudur Aled 99

Urban, Bp of Llandaff 20, 81–2, 117

Vikings 16–19, 26, 28–9, 31, 58, 61n, 67, 102, 115, 118, 123

wells, holy 25, 28, 79–80, 83, 112
Welsh language 15, 33, 78, 101, 105–6
William the Conqueror 19, 67, 88, 115
Winifred, St *see* Gwenfrewi, St
women, role in Church 58–9

Ynys Seiriol 25, 28
Ystradfellte 31, 42